Frommer's

D0447663

Amst

day BY day

4th Edition

by Sasha Heseltine

FrommerMedia LLC

Contents

Published by:

Frommer Media LLC

Frommer's is a trademark or registered trademark of Arthur Frommer.

ISBN: 978-1-628-87126-5 (paper); 978-1-628-87127-2 (ebk)

Editorial Director: Pauline Frommer
Editor: Michael Kelly
Production Editor: Carol Pogoni
Photo Editor: Ellen Herbert
Cartographer: Elizabeth Puhl
Indexer: Maro Riofrancos

Front cover photos, left to right: Red, pink, and yellow tulip fields isolated on a blue sky in the Netherlands, near Keukenhof, Lisse © Katoosha/Shutterstock; Canal house with windows with red shutters, Amsterdam © Katoosha/Shutterstock; *Self-Portrait with Felt Hat* (1888), Vincent van Gogh, Van Gogh Museum, Amsterdam © Georgios Makkas.

Back cover photo: The Damrak canal, Amsterdam © Anibal Trejo/Shutterstock.

For information on our other products and services, please go to Frommers.com.

Frommer's also publishes its books in a variety of electronic formats. Some content that appears in print may not be available in electronic formats.

Manufactured in China

5 4 3 2 1

About This Guide

Organizing your time. That's what this guide is all about.

Other guides give you long lists of things to see and do and then expect you to fit the pieces together. The Day by Day guides are different. These guides tell you the best of everything, and then they show you how to see it *in the smartest, most time-efficient way*. Our authors have designed detailed itineraries organized by time, neighborhood, or special interest. And each tour comes with a bulleted map that takes you from stop to stop.

Hoping to admire some Van Goghs, or buy some tulip bulbs to take back home? Planning to pedal along some canals, or take a whirlwind tour of the very best that Amsterdam has to offer? Whatever your interest or schedule, the Day by Days give you the smartest routes to follow. Not only do we take you to the top attractions, hotels, and restaurants, but we also help you access those special moments that locals get to experience—those "finds" that turn tourists into travelers.

The Day by Days are also your top choice if you're looking for one complete guide for all your travel needs. The best hotels and restaurants for every budget, the greatest shopping values, the wildest nightlife—it's all here.

Why should you trust our judgment? Because our authors personally visit each place they write about. They're an independent lot who say what they think and would never include places they wouldn't recommend to their best friends. They're also open to suggestions from readers. If you'd like to contact them, please send your comments our way at feedback@frommers.com, and we'll pass them on.

Enjoy your Day by Day guide—the most helpful travel companion you can buy. And have the trip of a lifetime.

About the Author

Sasha Heseltine has circled the globe, feeding orphaned wallabies on South Australia's Kangaroo Island, getting lost off-roading in the Sierra Nevada, diving with manta rays in the Maldives, and hot-air ballooning in eastern Poland. Back home in the U.K., she reviews hotels and restaurants for local media, and writes about her travels for international print and online publications.

An Additional Note

Please be advised that travel information is subject to change at any time—and this is especially true of prices. We therefore suggest that you write or call ahead for confirmation when making your travel plans. The authors, editors, and publisher cannot be held responsible for the experiences of readers while traveling. Your safety is important to us, however, so we encourage you to stay alert and be aware of your surroundings.

Star Ratings, Icons & Abbreviations

Every hotel, restaurant, and attraction listing in this guide has been ranked for quality, value, service, amenities, and special features using a **star-rating system.** Hotels, restaurants, attractions, shopping, and nightlife are rated on a scale of zero stars (recommended) to three stars (exceptional). In addition to the star-rating system, we also use a **kids icon** to point out the best bets for families. Within each tour, we recommend cafes, bars, or restaurants where you can take a break. Each of these stops appears in a shaded box marked with a coffee-cup-shaped bullet ☕.

Frommers.com

Now that you have this guidebook to help you plan a great trip, visit our website at **www.frommers.com** for additional travel information on more than 3,600 destinations. We update features regularly to give you instant access to the most current trip-planning information available. At Frommers.com, you'll find scoops on the best airfares, lodging rates, and car rental bargains. You can even book your travel online through our reliable travel-booking partners. Other popular features include:

- Online updates of our most popular guidebooks
- Vacation sweepstakes and contest giveaways
- Newsletters highlighting the hottest travel trends
- Online travel message boards with featured travel discussions

A Note on Prices

In the "Take a Break" and "Best Bets" sections of this book, we have used a system of dollar signs to show a range of costs for 1 night in a hotel (the price of a double-occupancy room) or the cost of an entree at a restaurant. Use the following table to decipher the dollar signs:

Cost	Hotels	Restaurants
$	under $100	under $10
$$	$100–$200	$10–$20
$$$	$200–$300	$20–$30
$$$$	$300–$400	$30–$40
$$$$$	over $400	over $40

An Invitation to the Reader

In researching this book, we discovered many wonderful places—hotels, restaurants, shops, and more. We're sure you'll find others. Please tell us about them, so we can share the information with your fellow travelers in upcoming editions. If you were disappointed with a recommendation, we'd love to know that, too. Please write to: Support@FrommerMedia.com.

13 Favorite
Moments

13 Favorite **Moments**

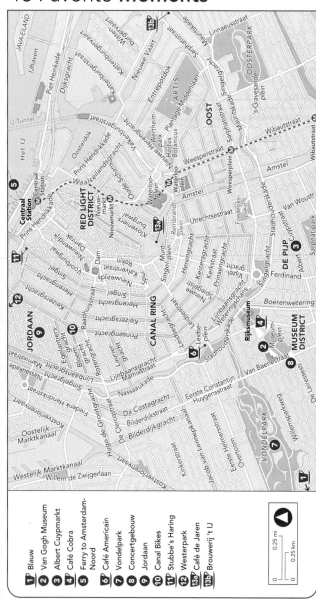

Previous page: One of Amsterdam's idyllic canals at dusk.

Amsterdam is a very special place. It has some of the most beautiful architecture in the world, a long history, and a vibrant multiracial community. Despite its pride in its roots, this is not a city that lives in the past. Innovative new buildings are going up at a blistering rate, the restaurant and nightlife scene is buzzing and ever-changing, and culturally it's open to (almost) anything. Here are a few of my favorite Amsterdam moments; experience some of these and you'll begin to grasp the psyche of this wonderful city.

❶ **Booking a table at Blauw,** the hottest new arrival on Amsterdam's Indonesian restaurant scene, for deliciously spicy rijstaffel and the buzzing, raucous atmosphere. Service is friendly, and the numerous dishes of saté, rices, pickles, salads, and curries are some of the best in town. *See p 15.*

❷ **Admiring the paintings at the Van Gogh Museum** late in the afternoon just before the museum closes is one of the highlights of a trip to Amsterdam. That's when the usually crowded second-floor gallery is almost empty, and you get the chance to admire Vincent's brush strokes without being shoved around by the throngs. *See p 13.*

You can see Van Gogh's self-portrait and many other famous works at the Van Gogh Museum.

❸ **Heading down to the Albert Cuypmarkt** early in the morning as the stalls on this long, multiethnic, and vibrant street are being laid out for a day of frantic shopping activity; this is a "real" Amsterdam moment and a chance to peek beyond the usual tourist confines. *See p 75.*

❹ **Sitting on the terrace at Café Cobra in Museumplein** on a sunny

Sunday afternoon to watch well-heeled local families relaxing over their champagne brunch. Dutch family life swirls around you as kids play on the swings and run through the low-level fountains to keep cool. *See p 8.*

❺ **Catching the ferry to Amsterdam-Noord (North)** from behind

Find fresh cheese, fish, fruit, vegetables, and more at the Albert Cuypmarkt.

Biking along Amsterdam's canals is a great way to get to know the city.

Centraal Station introduces a sense of where the future of Amsterdam lies. The narrow IJ waterway is full of boats, ferries, and barges, so catch the free ferry to the north bank to take in the views and the gleaming new architecture. *See p 41.*

6 Living the Americain Dream by taking coffee in the stunning Art Nouveau and Art Deco ambience of the Hampshire Amsterdam American Hotel's Café Americain. Guests will be relieved to learn that the service has improved considerably since a postwar Dutch writer dubbed the waiters here "unemployed knife throwers." *See p 85.*

7 Strolling in Vondelpark on a sunny afternoon feels like being a million miles from the city. The English-style park is an echo of the countryside translated to the city, and if you're lucky, you'll see the bright-green parakeets that have made the park their home. But do watch out for the cyclists. *See p 78.*

8 Dressing up for a classical concert at the Concertgebouw, the majestic neoclassical concert hall in Museumplein, is the best way to see middle-class Amsterdam out and about after dark. The acoustics

and the repertoire are among the very best in Europe. *See p 116.*

9 Strolling in the Jordaan, no matter the weather, to discover the beautiful tree-fringed canals, the narrow cobbled streets, the gabled houses, and the houseboats, and then stopping for a coffee at the neighborhood cafe 't Smalle. *See p 57.*

10 Peeking at houseboats at eye level as you pedal a canal bike around the Canal Ring allows you to see Amsterdam from a different perspective. *See p 82.*

11 Eating a raw herring with pickles and onions at Stubbe's Haring is all about sampling delicacies held dear to a Dutch native's heart. Don't dangle the fish by its tail over your mouth as that's considered to be very bad manners in Amsterdam. Chop it up and eat it with a fork. *See p 99.*

12 Catching an open-air rock concert in the Westerpark along with thousands of Amsterdammers and enjoying the relaxed vibe of the contemporary city at play. *See p 60.*

13 Sipping a white wine or a frothy Belgian beer in a waterside cafe as the sun goes down is surely everybody's favorite ending to a day sightseeing in Amsterdam. Try Café de Jaren on Nieuwe Doelenstraat or Brouwerij 't IJ on Funenkade. *See p 106 and p 110.* ●

Try some herring the way the locals eat it—with pickles and onions.

The Best **in One Day**

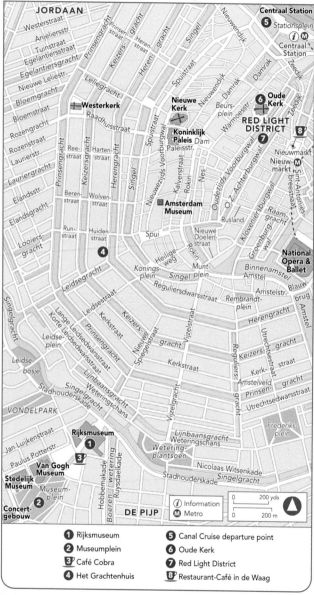

1. Rijksmuseum
2. Museumplein
3. Café Cobra
4. Het Grachtenhuis
5. Canal Cruise departure point
6. Oude Kerk
7. Red Light District
8. Restaurant-Café in de Waag

Previous page: Touring Amsterdam by canal boat can help you get a feel for the city.

Amsterdam was one of the most powerful cities in the world in the 17th century, when it experienced a period of great wealth and worldwide expansion. Understanding that history is vital to capturing the essence of this lovely city, so today's the day for getting to grips with the essentials. START: **Tram 2 or 5 to Rijksmuseum; Tram 12 to Museumplein; Tram 7 or 10 to Spiegelgracht.**

❶ ★★ Rijksmuseum. After a 10-year refurbishment, this grande old dame of the Amsterdam museum scene reopened in 2013. The Rijksmuseum, which opened in 1855, is the world's biggest repository of Dutch Golden Age treasures, four sprawling floors in the redbrick monolith designed by architect Pierre Cuypers (who

Vermeer's The Kitchen Maid, at the Rijksmuseum.

also designed **Centraal Station;** see p 29). The refurb spectacularly spruces up the elegant decorations in the central Voorhal (Great Hall), but the layout remains confusing. It saddens me to criticize this venerable institution, but the biggest mistake is crowding all the famous **Dutch Old Masters ★★★** together in the Gallery of Honour on the second floor. Around 2.3 million people visit this museum annually and they all want to see Rembrandt's *The Night Watch* and the wonderful works by Jan Steen, Jan Vermeer,

I amsterdam sign on Museumplein.

and Frans Hals, so prepare for impenetrable throngs. *The Milkmaid* and *The Merry Drinker* are truly mesmerizing, so bear with the crowds.

Elsewhere in the museum are glorious collections of tulip vases, fine silver and glassware, Delftware, Asian artifacts, and works by CoBrA artist Karel Appel and De Stijl designer Gerrit Rietveld. Don't forget the sculpture exhibitions in the gardens. Lines are always long, so reserve a ticket online before your visit or turn up right at opening time. And—like everywhere else in Amsterdam—watch out for bicyclists who stream through the museum's underpass. ⏱ *4 hr. Museumstraat 1.* ☎ *020/674-7000. www.rijksmuseum.nl. Admission 15€ adults, free for kids 18 and under. Daily 9am–5pm. Tram: 2 or 5 to Rijksmuseum, 12 to Museumplein, or 7 or 10 to Spiegelgracht.*

❷ ★★ Museumplein. After the crush of the Rijksmuseum, take a breather in the spacious Museumplein, home to the others in Amsterdam's triumvirate of great art museums, the **Van Gogh** (see p 13) and the **Stedelijk** (see p 19). The elaborate facade of **Het Concertgebouw** (see p 116) faces the Rijksmuseum across the piazza, which has become a buzzing public space with lawns, buskers, outdoor

I amsterdam City Card

This euro-saving sightseeing card provides free entry into most Amsterdam museums and free travel on public transport. It also entitles cardholders to a free canal cruise; discounts in certain stores and restaurants; admission to attractions outside Amsterdam, including **Zaanse Schans** and the museums in **Haarlem** (see p 136); a city map; and reduced admission to the Rijksmuseum. Prices in 2014: 47€ for 24 hours, 57€ for 48 hours, and 67€ for 72 hours. For more details or to buy online, go to www.iamsterdam.com.

cafes, museum stores, and a kids' playground. In winter, the area in front of the Rijksmuseum is transformed into a fairytale ice rink, backed by one of Amsterdam's iconic "I amsterdam" signs. ◷ *1 hr. Museumplein. Tram: 2 or 5 to Rijksmuseum, 12 to Museumplein, or 7 or 10 to Spiegelgracht.*

3 **Café Cobra.** Nothing beats sitting outside at Café Cobra on a sunny afternoon, watching the great and good of Amsterdam pass by across Museumplein. The food is not top-drawer but the spicy croquettes and *bitterballen* (meatballs) accompanied with fat fries, mayo, and a glass of *prosecco* certainly hit the spot. Inside, the cafe is heaving all day but the service is always impeccable and smooth. *Hobbemastraat 18.* ☎ *020/470-0111. www.cobracafe.nl. $$.*

4 ★★★ **Het Grachtenhuis (Canal Museum).** Take the tram to Herengracht on the Grachtengordel (Canal Ring) to the elegant mansion housing the Canal Museum. This excellent museum highlights Amsterdam's expansion through a brilliantly curated series of interactive displays. First, a sound-and-light show centers on a model of the city in medieval times; it was

grim and overcrowded, with little concession to hygiene. By the 17th century, growth became imperative. The planning and construction of the ring of three canals around the medieval city is described in a lively series of interactive displays, films, models, and holograms; the final exhibit is an all-singing, all-dancing celebration of multicultural Amsterdam today. You couldn't find a more entertaining introduction to the city. ◷ *1 hr. Herengracht 386.* ☎ *020/421-1656. www.hetgrachtenhuis.nl. Admission 12€ adults, 6€ ages 6–17. Tues–Sun 10am–5pm. Closed Mon. Tram: 2 or 5 to Koningsplein.*

5 ★★ **Canal Cruise.** Take the tram from Leidsestraat up to Centraal Station, head to the left of the building, and get in line for the Holland International Canal Cruise, free with the I amsterdam City Card. There's no better way to discover Amsterdam than from its waterways. Cruises loop northwards into the IJ, bordered by the gleaming contemporary architecture of **EYE Film Institute** (see p 29) and **Science Center NEMO** (see p 34), before entering the Canal Ring and passing along the eastern canals, giving sight of the Magere Brug (Skinny Bridge). Then it's up Herengracht past mighty mansions and the "nine bridges" viewpoint. There's a (sometimes lackluster) commentary

The Oude Kerk (Old Church).

in English. ⏱ *1 hr. Prins Hendrikkade 33A.* ☎ *020/217-0501. Cruises leave every 30 min. Ticket 15€. Tram: 1, 2, or 5 to Centraal Station.*

⑥ ★★ Oude Kerk (Old Church).

This late-Gothic, triple-nave church was begun in 1250 and completed with the extension of the bell tower in 1566. Its exterior is encrusted with 17th- and 18th-century houses, and the barnlike interior was stripped of all its adornment in the Alteration of 1578, when practicing Catholicism was banned. Rembrandt's beloved first wife lies in vault 28K, which bears the simple inscription SASKIA JUNI 1642. The magnificent 1728 organ is regularly used for recitals. On a guided tour, you can climb the church tower for a great view of central Amsterdam and the Red Light District (Apr–Sept only, Thurs–Sat 1–5pm). ⏱ *30 min. Oudekerksplein 23.* ☎ *020/625-8284 church;*

020/689-2565 tower. www.oudekerk. nl. Church: Admission 7.50€ adults; 5€ seniors, students, and kids 13–18. Mon–Sat 10am–6pm; Sun 1–5:30pm. Closed Jan 1, Apr 27, and Dec 25. Metro: Nieuwmarkt.

⑦ ★★★ Red Light District.

A step away from the Oude Kerk and you're immersed in the seedy underbelly of Amsterdam's Red Light District, where barely clad prostitutes advertise themselves behind glass windows along the medieval canals and alleyways. There are also live, hard-core sex shows (see p 118) that leave nothing to the imagination. Although the area is generally safe, **a word of warning:** Don't photograph the prostitutes; it might be tempting to take pictures of half-naked women posing in windows but it is not appreciated. ⏱ *30 min. Dusk is the best time to visit, though it's open 24 hr. Metro: Nieuwmarkt.*

⑧ Restaurant-Café in de Waag.

Bang in the middle of vibrant Nieuwmarkt, the historic Waag buzzes day and night; its outdoor cafe is filled to bursting all afternoon and it serves late-night snacks of nachos and Dutch cheeses to soak up any surfeits of alcohol. *Nieuwmarkt 4.* ☎ *020/422-7772. www.indewaag.nl. $$.*

The Red Light District at night.

The Best **in Two Days**

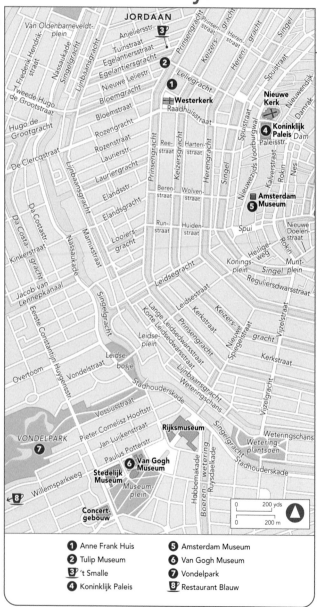

1 Anne Frank Huis	**5** Amsterdam Museum
2 Tulip Museum	**6** Van Gogh Museum
3 't Smalle	**7** Vondelpark
4 Koninklijk Paleis	**8** Restaurant Blauw

msterdam is famous for many things apart from canals and prostitutes, including Anne Frank, Van Gogh, tulips, the nationwide adoration of its royal family, and pride in its past. Today you'll dig further into the city's psyche with visits to royal palaces and heavyweight museums. START: **Tram 13, 14, or 17 to Westermarkt.**

The bookcase door that led to Anne Frank's hiding place.

❶ ★★★ **Anne Frank Huis.** If you don't want to wait for hours for admission to this nondescript canal house, apply for tickets online about a month before your visit. This is one of Amsterdam's most popular sights, for the insights it provides into the incarceration of 13-year-old Anne Frank and her Jewish family during the Nazi occupation of Amsterdam in World War II. This would have gone largely unmarked had she not written a diary of her time in the secret attic, which was published by her father after her death. Otto Frank took his family and other Jewish refugees into hiding behind his jam-making

factory on July 6, 1942; they remained there for 2 years until they were betrayed to the Nazis and deported, Anne to Bergen-Belsen in Germany and her parents to Auschwitz in Poland. Along with her sister, Anne died of typhus just months before Liberation, and only their father survived the war.

The apartments where the family hid carry sad reminders of their life there: the posters Anne put up to decorate her bedroom; the height marks against the wall; the steep, creaking stairs; and the claustrophobic rooms. Sound bites from her diary and a heartrending final word from her father augment the somber atmosphere. Despite the crowds, this haunting museum has the power to silence everyone. ⏱ *90 min. Prinsengracht 263–267.* ☎ *020/556-7100. www.annefrank. org. Admission 9€ adults, 4.50€ kids 10–17. Nov–Mar Sun–Fri 9am–7pm, Sat 9am–9pm; Apr–Jun, Sept–Oct Sun–Fri 9am–9pm, Sat 9am–10pm; Jul–Aug daily 9am–10pm. Closed Yom Kippur. Tram: 13, 14, or 17 to Westermarkt.*

❷ ★★ **Tulip Museum.** The perfect antidote after a viewing of the Anne Frank Huis, the revamped Tulip Museum across the Prinsengracht is cheery, contemporary, and informative on the story of Amsterdam's obsession with tulips, which arrived from the Himalayas and nearly brought the country down when trade in the bulbs collapsed in 1637 (see p 14). It's all showcased in a short, well-designed exhibition,

Koninklijk Paleis (Royal Palace).

with fantastic images and bright displays. Upstairs is a top-quality souvenir store selling bulbs and other quality tulip-related ephemera. ⏱ *45 min. Prinsengracht 116.* ☎ *020/421-0095. www.amsterdam tulipmuseum.com. Admission 6€ adults, 4€ students. Daily 10am–6pm. Closed Apr 27 and Dec 25. Tram: 13, 14, or 17 to Westermarkt.*

3 ★★★ **'t Smalle.** On the edge of the cute Jordaan area, 't Smalle is a traditional locals' cafe decked out in wood and glass and offering a small menu of snacks. The primary business here is the beer, so grab a glass and sit outside on the decking over the canal. *Egelantiersgracht 12.* ☎ *020/623-9617. www.t-smalle.nl. $.*

4 ★★ **Koninklijk Paleis (Royal Palace).** Navigate the alleyways of Amsterdam's old center to the Dam. The huge building in the middle of Amsterdam's main square is the official residence of the

reigning Dutch House of Orange, although these days they prefer to reside in The Hague. The palace was designed by Jacob van Campen in 1655 as the City Hall and has a solid, neoclassical facade; it was repurposed into a royal palace by Louis, brother of Napoleon Bonaparte, when he became king in 1806. Its public rooms are now open to view. The interior is crammed with early-19th-century furniture, chandeliers, sculptures, and vast oil paintings reflecting Amsterdam's wealth during the Golden Age. Highlights include the ornate Council Chamber and the high-ceilinged Burgerzaal, where maps inlaid on the marble floors show Amsterdam as the center of the world. The palace is closed to visitors during periods of royal residence and state receptions. ⏱ *1 hr. Dam.* ☎ *020/620-4060. www.paleisamsterdam.nl. Admission 10€ adults, 9€ seniors and students, free for kids 17 and under. Daily 11am–5pm (check on the website before visiting as there are frequent changes and closures). Tram: 4, 9, 16, or 24 to Dam.*

5 ★★ **Amsterdam Museum.** It's a lively walk through the boutiques of the **Negen Straatjes** (Nine Streets; see p 55) down to the city's historical museum. The museum is housed partly in a former convent and partly in a 17th-century orphanage and is pleasantly sited around a cobbled courtyard. Telling the story of Amsterdam's progression from simple fishing village to world power, the displays kick off superbly with the interactive exhibition Amsterdam DNA, which takes a whistle-stop tour through the main stages of the city's history using Old Dutch

The Dutch Royal Family

Although King Willem-Alexander's official home is the Koninklijk Paleis, like his other residences, it is owned by the Dutch state, which allocates a budget of about 37 million euros per year to manage the royal household. He was invested as king of The Netherlands on April 30, 2013—on what was Queen's Day—when his mother Queen Beatrix abdicated in his favor. He is married to the Spanish Princess Máxima, and they have three daughters. The king is a constitutional monarch, and the Dutch Royal Family dates back to William of Orange (1533–1584, also king of England), which is why the Dutch always wear orange for national celebrations.

Master paintings, maps, tools, armor, and religious sculpture. After that, things tail off as you are led through gallery after gallery of poorly organized artifacts; one highlight is the 1677 scale model of the Koninklijk Paleis. The **Schuttersgalerij** (Civic Guards Gallery; see p 25) outside the museum leads between Kalverstraat and the Begijnhof (see p 49). Along with the massive wooden sculptures of David and Goliath, a nice touch here is the 40m (131 ft.) tapestry created by Barbara Broekman to represent the 179 nationalities living in Amsterdam. ① *2 hr. Kalverstraat 92.* ☎ *020/523-1822. www. amsterdammuseum.nl. Admission 11€ adults, 5€ kids 5–18. Daily 10am–5pm. Closed Apr 27 and Dec 25. Tram: 1, 2, or 5 to Spui.*

⑥ ★★★ Van Gogh Museum

Several tram routes stop near Museumplein for the second of Amsterdam's artistic heavyweights. At press time, the Van Gogh

An exhibit from the Amsterdam Museum.

Tulip Madness at Keukenhof Gardens

Tulip mania hit Amsterdam in the 1630s, when the prized bulbs were imported from Asia and changed hands for astronomical amounts of money. The market abruptly collapsed in 1637, but the tulip is still critical to Holland today, with the country producing 75% of the world's tulip bulbs. Tourists fly in every spring to view the billions of bulbs in the Bollenstreek (bulb region) southwest of Amsterdam between Leiden and Haarlem, where the bulbs thrive on fertile sandy soil backed by the North Sea dunes. The biggest, brightest tulip show of all is found in Keukenhof Gardens (www.keukenhof.nl) near Lisse, where seven million daffodils, hyacinths, crocuses, and tulips burst into bloom in April, forming psychedelic swathes among the trees and pathways of the world-famous gardens. The gardens are open only from late March to mid-May for guided tours and trips through the surrounding bulb fields by electric boat. If you buy bulbs to take out of the country, make sure they are stamped for export on the packet.

Museum was being expanded, but it's still very much open for business. The museum opened in 1973, designed by Gerrit Rietveld, leading exponent of the De Stijl movement; it has three floors of white, airy space in which to show off the tortured artist's ethereal works to their best advantage. Vincent van Gogh was born in 1853 in Groot-Zundert in the south of Holland, and during his short life, he produced over 800 paintings. More than 200 of his portraits, landscapes, and still lifes, plus 500 drawings, are held here, forming the biggest Van Gogh collection in the world. Displays start with various works from different points in Vincent's career hung alongside contemporary works by Pissarro, Gauguin, and Monet to provide historical context.

The exhibition on the second floor shows the artist finding his way stylistically, and this is where you'll see Van Gogh's seminal paintings as his career is tracked from his early still lifes through his Japanese stage to his untimely death at Arles in 1890. Van Gogh was extraordinarily prolific in his last years, and world-famous examples of his brilliance on display here include the gloomy *Potato Eaters* (1885), *Bedroom at Arles* (1888), and an 1889 version of *Sunflowers*. The museum's grand new entrance is set to open summer 2015.
🕐 *2 hr. Paulus Potterstraat 7.*
☎ *020/570-5200. www.vangogh museum.nl. Admission 15€ adults, free for kids 16 and under. Daily Mar 1–Sept 1, Dec 27–Dec 31 9am–6pm; Sept 2–Dec 26 9am–5pm; Fri open until 10pm year-round. Tram: 2, 3, 5, or 12 to Van Baerlestraat; 16 or 24 to Museumplein.*

Avid shoppers will want to head to P.C. Hoofstraat for upscale shops and boutiques.

7 ★★ **Vondelpark.** A 5-minute stroll from the Van Gogh down Van Baerlestraat (wander down to **P.C. Hoofstraat** to gawk at the expensive stores) brings you to Amsterdam's biggest, greenest public park, providing 44 hectares (109 acres) of peace and quiet. This cherished open space is crammed with trees, lawns, lakes, and bridges criss-crossed with walking, biking, and jogging tracks, although as usual cyclists take

Vondelpark is the perfect place to relax on a sunny day.

precedence, so watch your step. Summer sees the lakeside restaurants filling up and the draw of open-air festivals and concerts (see p 116). ⏱ *30 min. Enter through the gate on Van Eeghenlaan, at the corner of Jacob Obrechtstraat. Open 24 hr. Tram: 2, 3, 5, or 12 to Van Baerlestraat.*

8 **Restaurant Blauw.** A 30-minute hike through the Vondelpark ends up on Amstelveenseweg and at this amazing modern Indonesian restaurant, which is filled to the rafters on two noisy floors every night. The *rijsttafel* consists of an amazing 17 dishes including pickles; fried and sticky rice; pork balls; plantain; saté; and beef, pork, chicken, and fish dishes. Heaven. *Amstelveenseweg 158–160.* ☎ *020/675-5000. www. restaurantblauw.nl. $$$.*

The Best **in Three Days**

1. Hermitage Amsterdam
2. Waterlooplein Flea Market
3. Café de Sluyswacht
4. Museum Het Rembrandthuis
5. Bloemenmarkt
6. Stedelijk Museum
7. Heineken Experience
8. Miss Korea

More Amsterdam icons today, Rembrandt and Heineken included. So get ready for a day of mixing and matching, mooching around markets, and encountering more great art before rewarding yourself with a glass or two of fine Dutch beer at the end of the day. START: **Tram 9 or 14 to Waterlooplein.**

1 ★★ **Hermitage Amsterdam.** The Amsterdam branch of St. Petersburg's Hermitage is a delight to visit; it's housed in the Amstelhof, a former almshouse (see p 50) for elderly women built in 1680 behind a serene neoclassical facade. Centered on a giant courtyard and all but surrounded by canals and the Amstel River, the building has been beautifully transformed into a state-of-the-art gallery displaying the rich offerings from the Russian state collection. Two exhibitions run simultaneously for about 6 months. Check online before you visit but with the Hermitage holding more than 3 million works of art, chances are the current exhibition will be spectacular. ① *2 hr. Amstel 51.* ☎ *020/530-7488. www.hermitageamsterdam.nl. Admission 15€ adults, 12€ seniors and students, 5€ kids 6–16. Daily 10am–5pm. Closed Apr 27 and Dec 25. Tram: 9 or 14 to Waterlooplein.*

2 ★ **Waterlooplein Flea Market.** A 5-minute walk from the Hermitage along the Amstel leads to

You'll find lots of Dutch wares, like these mini porcelain clogs, at the Waterlooplein Flea Market.

the city's best-known flea market. Two canals were filled in 1882 to form a market square that by 1893 lay at the heart of the Jewish Quarter. Before World War II, it was a daily market central to Jewish life, but as Amsterdam's Jews were deported, it fell into disrepair. During the 1960s, the market was reborn when dazed hippies floated in from all over Europe in the haze of their summer of love to sell bongs and water pipes. Today the

Amsterdam Facts & Figures

In Amsterdam, you'll find 800,000 permanent residents and more than a million visitors each month, who visit more than 40 museums. Much of the city is under sea level; its inhabitants own more than 1.2 million bicycles and come from 179 different nationalities. The city boasts 165 canals crossed by 1,281 bridges, and the Grachtengordel (Canal Ring) was listed as a World Heritage site by UNESCO in 2010. Amsterdam has 8 functioning windmills and owns 22 paintings by Rembrandt.

A room in the Museum Het Rembrandthuis (Rembrandt House Museum).

market has around 300 stalls flogging anything from knock-off DVDs to piles of vintage clothes, plastic jewelry, and (ironically) Nazi pilot leather jackets. If you take time to scrabble deeply around the stalls, you may even find some decent secondhand books. ⓘ *30 min. Waterlooplein 2. www.waterloopleinmarkt.nl. Mon–Fri 9am–5:30pm, Sat 8:30am–5:30pm. Tram: 9 or 14 to Waterlooplein.*

3 ⓑ Café de Sluyswacht. Tilting at a precarious angle, this former 17th-century lock-keeper's cottage is one of the oldest and most famous pubs in Amsterdam. Inside all is crooked, with wooden bars and uneven stone floors. Sample the *wit bier* and a plate of strong Dutch cheese and enjoy the tiny terraces with views over Oudeschans canal or the Rembrandthuis. *Jodenbreestraat 1. ☎ 020/625-7611. www.sluyswacht.nl. $.*

4 ★★★ Museum Het Rembrandthuis. Just opposite Café de Sluyswacht is the former home of Rembrandt van Rijn, Dutch artist

extraordinaire. He bought this elegant townhouse in 1639 when his career as Amsterdam's premier portrait painter was flying, and he overstretched himself with a massive mortgage that plagued his life for years. The house brought him little personal happiness as his adored first wife Saskia died here in 1642 and then he was declared bankrupt in 1656. Rembrandt's belongings were all sold off and he moved to a smaller house on Rozengracht, where he died in 1669. The house reopened as a museum in 1911, and the layout of the house is typical of the 17th century, with servants' quarters in the basement and three floors atop this. Rembrandt's hallway served as his gallery, and the family's living quarters are hung with his masterly oil paintings. Upstairs you'll find his cabinet of curiosities and the airy studio where he painted *The Night Watch*. Bequests of his prints and paintings continue to grow, and in 1998 a new wing was built to display them all. ⓘ *1 hr. Jodenbreestraat 4.*

You'll find a large variety of flowers, including lots of tulips, at the Bloemenmarkt.

50 tulpen
€ 7.50

☎ 020/520-0400. www.
rembrandthuis.nl. Admission 13€
adults, 10€ students, 4€ kids 6–17.
Daily 10am–6pm. Closed Apr 27 and
Dec 25. Tram: 9 or 14 to
Waterlooplein.

❺ ★★ **Bloemenmarkt (Flower
Market).** Catch tram 9 or 14 from
Waterlooplein or walk along the
River Amstel to Amsterdam's last
remaining floating market and the
world's only floating flower market.
This explosion of color is now a
permanent fixture housed on a row
of moored barges. Here you'll also
find seeds, bulbs, gardening tools,
and houseplants. Yes, these days
it's touristy but the seasonal displays are always a pleasure to look
at, especially over Christmas and
during the spring when the stalls
burst with riots of bright blooms.
🕐 30 min. Singel. Mon–Sat 9am–
5:30pm, Sun 11am–5:30pm. Tram: 4,
9, 14, 16, or 24 to Muntplein.

❻ ★★★ **Stedelijk.** Jump on
tram 16 or 24 from Muntplein; dev-
otees of contemporary art will fall in
love with this museum. The original
1895 building by A. W. Weissman
has been renovated and a curious
bath-like extension has been
appended to its flank, which now
houses temporary exhibitions. The
interior is bright, white, and airy, all
the better to show off its stellar collections of works by the most
famous names of the 19th to 21st
centuries. Things get off to an
excellent start with the vibrant
mural by Karel Appel in the first
gallery, which sparkles in the sun;
the roster of great artists exhibited
include Mondriaan, Chagall, Van
Gogh, Spencer, Matta, Newman,
Pollock, and pop artists Warhol and
Lichtenstein. The museum's design
collection is less successful as the
layout is cramped, but there are
many stand-out pieces here,

An exhibit from the Stedelijk Museum.

including Gerrit Rietveld's famous
painted Chair and Jeff Koons's
kitsch Ushering in Banality (1988).
Everyone's going to have their
favorite piece among all this
genius; mine is the gigantic tapestry Hollywood Crinkle (2010) by Pae
White, which glistens like candy
wrappers. 🕐 2 hr. Museumplein 10.
☎ 020/573-2911. www.stedelijk.nl.
Daily 10am–6pm (Thurs until 10pm).
Admission 15€ adults, 7.50€ students, free for kids 18 and under.
Tram: 2, 3, 5, or 12 to Van Baerlestraat; 16 or 24 to Museumplein.

❼ ★★ **Heineken Experience.**
Take the 15-minute stroll across
Museumplein or get tram 16 or 24
to one of the most popular draws
in Amsterdam. The Heineken is
always crowded with multinational
youngsters eager to get their hands
on some beer. It's housed inside

Visitors examine a copper brewing kettle
at the Heineken Experience.

the red-brick former brewery, which functioned from 1867 until 1988 before production was moved to modern facilities in The Hague and Den Bosch. The intro to Heineken, delivered by human hologram from behind a well-stocked bar, sets the pace for a rollicking journey through the growth of the brand from microbrewery to a multi-million-euro, international company with liberal use of interactive exhibits and funny simulated rides. The tour also incorporates the original copper brewing vats, malt silos, and vintage brewing equipment, plus a stable full of Shire horses used to pull the promotional drays. The ultimate goal for most is to chug back Heineken beer at the bar. ○ *90 min. Stadhouderskade 78.*

☎ *020/523-9435. www.heineken experience.com. Admission 18€ adults (includes 2 beers), 13€ kids 12–17. Sept–June Mon–Thurs 11am–7:30pm, Fri–Sun 10:30am–9pm; Jul–Aug daily 10:30am–9pm. Tram: 16 or 24 to Stadhouderskade.*

8 ★★★ **Miss Korea Barbecue.** De Pijp is known for its multi-ethnic restaurants, so try something new. Barbecue your choice of meats, seafood, or poultry at the table and add side dishes from an array of rices, noodles, salads, *kimchi*, and dumplings. Desserts stretch only to ice cream but the BBQ is the reason to visit this packed, fun-filled restaurant. *Albert Cuypstraat 66–70.* ☎ *020/ 679-0606. www.misskorea.nl. $$.*

Photographic Galleries

Amsterdam is not just about Old Master paintings and contemporary art; there are plenty of options for photography lovers as well. The **FOAM Photography Museum** (see p 25) runs hard-hitting exhibitions in a modern gallery behind a traditional town house facade at Keizersgracht 609. Images are all beautifully displayed against pristine white walls, and displays change regularly. Check online to see what's on when you are in town; there are regular workshops, some especially for children. Also on Keizersgracht at 401 is the **Huis Marseille** (see p 25), another gallery specializing in contemporary photography, based in a former merchant's house. It's named for the stone plaque on the front of the building, which depicts the harbor in Marseille, France. ●

Amsterdam for Art Lovers

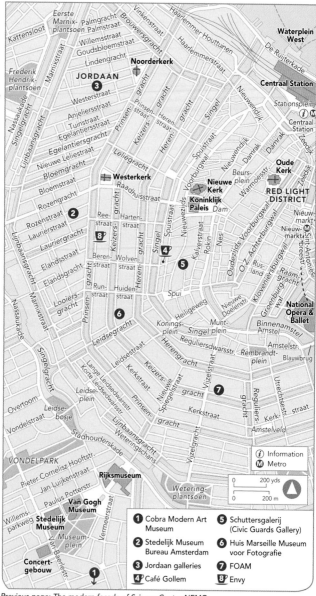

1 Cobra Modern Art Museum

2 Stedelijk Museum Bureau Amsterdam

3 Jordaan galleries

4 Café Gollem

5 Schuttersgalerij (Civic Guards Gallery)

6 Huis Marseille Museum voor Fotografie

7 FOAM

8 Envy

Previous page: The modern facade of Science Center NEMO.

msterdam is a feast for art lovers. With more than 20 Rembrandts, more than 200 Van Goghs, numerous Vermeers, and a plethora of Impressionist and post-Impressionist paintings scattered throughout the city, art lovers will be in heaven here. This tour is for art lovers who would have already made a beeline to the top museums and are ready to dig deeper into all the art riches that Amsterdam has to offer. Today, you'll have a chance to see contemporary works by local, living artists; the Stedelijk Museum's stylish off-shoot in the Jordaan; and the Schuttersgalerij, with its outsized canvases depicting well-to-do members of 17th-century Civic Guards companies. START: **Cobra Modern Art Museum; tram 5 to Amstelveen Binnenhof or Metro line 51 to Amstelveen Centrum.**

An exhibit from the Cobra Museum.

1 ★★ Cobra Modern Art Museum. Art lovers will find this breathtakingly contemporary museum worth the trek to its off-the-beaten-path location. The most enjoyable way to get here is the 20-minute tram 5 ride from Amsterdam city center, giving you a chance to see leafy, suburban Amstelveen as you rattle through the streets. The museum is a light-filled brick-and-glass affair with plenty of white space for framing the artwork; it was designed by

Dutch architect Wim Quist and opened in 1995. The collection overflows with the post–World War II abstract expressionist art and ceramics of the short-lived CoBrA Group, named for the initials of the founding artists' home cities: Copenhagen, Brussels, and Amsterdam. Karel Appel (1921–2006) and Constant (1920–2005) were the Dutch proponents, both controversial painters, sculptors, and ceramicists whose work, like their fellow CoBrA artists, has a childlike

An exhibit from the SMBA.

quality, employing strong colors and abstract shapes, as seen in Constant's oil painting *Figure of the Night* and Appel's delightfully simple ceramics. ⏱ *2 hr. Sandbergplein 1, Amstelveen.* ☎ *020/547-5050. www.cobra-museum.nl. Admission 9.50€ adults; 6€ seniors, students, and kids 6–18. Daily 10am–5pm. Closed Jan 1, Apr 27, and Dec 25. Tram: 5 to Amstelveen Binnenhof. Metro: Line 51 to Amstelveen Centrum.*

❷ ★★ Stedelijk Museum Bureau Amsterdam (SMBA). Catch tram 5 back to Spui and walk along Raadhuisstraat, passing the Westerkerk on your left. Cross Prinsengracht and turn left; take the first right to visit this mini-version of the **Stedelijk Museum** (see p 19), an innovative gallery designed to give a leg up to the careers of promising Amsterdam artists. Described in a Dutch newspaper as a "hatchery for young artistic talent," the gallery has a bland, white exhibition space perfect for showing off oft-changing exhibitions of photography, video, abstract works, installations, and occasionally intense performance art. ⏱ *45 min. Rozenstraat 59.* ☎ *020/422-0471. www.smba.nl. Free admission. Wed–Sun 11am–5pm. Closed Jan 1, Apr 27, and Dec 25–26. Tram: 13, 14, or 17 to Westermarkt.*

❸ ★ Galleries Around the Jordaan. You're in pretty Jordaan (see p 57) where narrow cobbled streets—and even narrower canals—are crammed with around 40 specialist art galleries. Check out Diana Stigter's eponymous gallery (Elandsstraat 90); she is reckoned to have her finger on the pulse of what's hot and what's not. GO Gallery (Prinsengracht 64) promotes street art, and the Edouard Planting Gallery (Eerste Bloemdwarsstraat 2) exhibits contemporary photography. ⏱ *30 min. Jordaan. Tram: 13, 14, or 17 to Westermarkt.*

4 ★★ Café Gollem. A traditional, cozy pub with a reputation for serving fine Belgian beers. Food plays second fiddle to the alcohol here, but is of the wholesome snacky variety, including vast cheese platters to soak up the beer. *Raamsteeg 4.* ☎ *020/612-9444. http://cafegollem.nl. $.*

5 ★ Schuttersgalerij (Civic Guards Gallery). Take the tram from the Westerkerk back to Spui and walk down to the **Amsterdam Museum** (see p 12). Outside the entrance, a narrow, glass-roofed walkway links Kalverstraat to the **Begijnhof** (see p 49). Displayed in the gallery are 15 bigger-is-better, 17th-century paintings showing the city's heroic musketeers, the Civic Guards. Elegantly uniformed and coiffed, these militia companies once played an important role in the city's defense, but degenerated into little more than banqueting societies. Their portraits are accompanied by a huge wooden sculpture of Goliath and a miniscule David, plus photographs of Amsterdam's contemporary elite side by side with the magical Barbara Broekman carpet representing the 179 nationalities of Amsterdam. ① *20 min. At Amsterdam Museum, Kalverstraat 92.* ☎ *020/523-1822. www.amsterdammuseum.nl. Free admission. Daily 10am–5pm. Closed Apr 27 and Dec 25. Tram: 1, 2, or 5 to Spui.*

6 ★★ Huis Marseille Museum voor Fotografie. Cross the Singel on to Herengracht and turn left. If you haven't already been, go to **Het Grachtenhuis** (the Canal Museum; see p 8) to learn about the expansion of Amsterdam's

canals in a truly engaging museum. Turn right onto Keizersgracht for Amsterdam's original photography museum, housed in an aristocratic merchant's house. Here, oft-changing photography exhibitions showcase contemporary images in pared-back galleries retaining some original features. ① *30 min. Keizersgracht 401.* ☎ *020/531-8989. www.huismarseille.nl. Admission 8€ adults, 4€ seniors and students, free for kids 17 and under. Tues–Sun 11am–6pm. Closed Jan 1, Apr 27, and Dec 25. Tram: 1, 2, or 5 to Keizersgracht.*

7 ★★★ FOAM. Further down Keizersgracht and opposite **Museum Van Loon** (see p 28), FOAM is another gallery dedicated to photography, tucked behind a traditional canal-house facade. Its interior has been partly stripped out to reveal a warren of white exhibition rooms that are the perfect backdrop to show off the work of established photographers, such as the highly graphic, intensely colored war images of U.S. photographer Richard Mosse or the work of newly discovered Dutch talent. ① *1 hr. Keizersgracht 609.* ☎ *020/ 551-6500. www.foam.org. Admission 9.50€ adults, 7€ seniors and students, free for kids 11 and under. Sat–Wed 10am–6pm, Thurs–Fri 10am–9pm. Closed Apr 27. Tram: 16 or 24 to Keizersgracht.*

8 ★★★ Envy. A sleek, new spot on the canalside, with an open kitchen to watch the chefs cook up a stylish modern-Italian storm with set menus or à la carte options. The venue is having a moment among Amsterdam's fickle fashionistas. *Prinsengracht 381.* ☎ *020/344-6407. www.envy.nl. $$$.*

Architectural **Amsterdam**

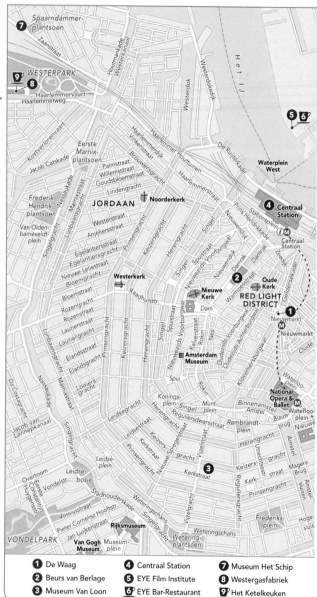

1 De Waag

2 Beurs van Berlage

3 Museum Van Loon

4 Centraal Station

5 EYE Film Institute

6 EYE Bar-Restaurant

7 Museum Het Schip

8 Westergasfabriek

9 Het Ketelkeuken

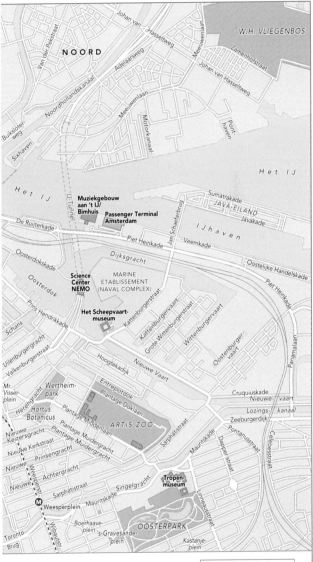

NOORD

W. H. VLIEGENBOS

Johan van Hasseltweg

Van der Pekstraat

Adelaarsweg

Noordhollandskanaal

Zamenhofstraat

Johan van Hasseltweg

Meeuwenlaan

Buiksloter-weg

Meeuwenlaan

Motorkanaal

Sixhaven

Pont-haven

Het IJ

Het IJ

IJ Tunnel

Muziekgebouw aan 't IJ/ Bimhuis

Sumatrakade
JAVA-EILAND
Javakade

Passenger Terminal Amsterdam

De Ruijterkade

Piet Heinkade

Jan Schaeferbrug

IJhaven

Veemkade

Oosterdokskade

Dijksgracht

Oostelijke Handelskade

Piet Heinkade

Oosterdok

Science Center NEMO

MARINE ETABLISSEMENT (NAVAL COMPLEX)

Prins Hendrikkade

Het Scheepvaart-museum

Kattenburgerstraat

Kattenburgervaart

Grote Wittenburgerstraat

Wittenburgervaart

Oostenburger-vaart

Panamalaan

Schans

Uilenburgergracht

Valkenburgerstraat

Hoogtekadijk

Nieuwe Vaart

Mr. Visser-plein

Wertheim-park

Entrepotdok

Cruquiuskade
Nieuwe- vaart

Herengracht

Hortus Botanicus

Plantage Doklaan

Plantage Middenlaan

Lozings- kanaal

Zeeburgerdijk

Pontanusstraat

Celebesstraat

Nieuwe Keizersgracht

Plantage Muiderlaan

ARTIS ZOO

Sarphatistraat

Nieuwe Kerkstraat

Plantage Muidergracht

Mauritskade

Dapperstraat

Prinsengracht

Nieuwe Achtergracht

Tropen-museum

Singelgracht

Weesperstraat

Wibautstr.

Sarphatistraat

Mauritskade

Linnaeusstraat

Ⓜ Weesperplein

Boerhaave-plein

's-Gravesande-plein

OOSTERPARK

Kastanje-plein

Toronto Brug

There are so many architectural styles in Amsterdam that the city can seem quite schizophrenic. Architecture buffs can entertain themselves just by walking the streets or taking a tram ride or canal trip, especially in the UNESCO-listed Grachtengordel (Canal Ring). On this tour, you'll get an overview of the major phases of architecture, from medieval to present-day icons. START: **Metro to Nieuwmarkt.**

❶ ★★ De Waag. On the fringe of Amsterdam's Chinatown, you'll find the city's only surviving medieval fortified gate. Built in the 14th century, it became a public weigh house and then a guild house. One of the guilds lodged here was the Surgeon's Guild, immortalized in Rembrandt's painting *The Anatomy Lesson* (1632), which depicts a dissection being conducted in the upper-floor Theatrum Anatomicum. This part of the building is rarely open, but you can dine in the historic ground-floor restaurant In de Waag (see p 52). ⏱ *15 min. Nieuwmarkt. Metro: Nieuwmarkt.*

De Waag.

❷ ★★ Beurs van Berlage. Walk through the Red Light District, which has some fine gabled architecture to offer, to Amsterdam's former stock exchange, built in 1903 by Hendrik Berlage and now a concert venue (see p 116). This monumental building was one of the precursors of the Amsterdam School architectural style and is exceptional for its use of patterned brickwork and clean lines, which broke away from the fancy Dutch Revivalist styles of

The exquisite garden of the Museum Van Loon.

the time as seen at the **Stedelijk Museum** (see p 19). A frieze decorates the facade of the building showing man's (questionable) evolution from Adam to stockbroker. ⏱ *10 min. Beursplein 1.* ☎ *020/ 530-4141. www.beursvanberlage.nl. Tram: 4, 9, 16, or 24 to the Dam.*

❸ ★ Museum Van Loon. Catch the tram to Keizersgracht. The Museum Van Loon is an elegant mansion first owned by Ferdinand Bol, a student of Rembrandt. Between 1884 and 1945, it was the property of the Van Loons, who were founders of the Dutch East India Company and one of the richest families in Amsterdam. Although this is a beautiful house with a double frontage as befits the family's wealth, its grand rooms have a vague air of neglect. However, it's worth a visit to see how the Dutch aristocracy lived among scores of family portraits (but not the ghastly modern ones upstairs by Katinka Lampe), the Louis

Amsterdam & the Sea

Amsterdam lies below sea level. That it does not lie beneath the sea itself is due to Dutch engineering skill, which has kept the city above water for the past 800 years. But still the solid buildings stand, even though they are 5.5m (18 ft.) below sea level, and its 800,000 inhabitants live where waves should by all rights be lapping. If the seacoast defenses—a complicated system of dams, polders, dykes, and defense walls—should ever be breached, most of the city would vanish beneath the waves. A cross-section of the topography between the North Sea and Amsterdam shows that the Vondelpark would become a lake, the Metro tunnels would be drowned, and the trams would float away. However, if you were standing on top of the Oude Kerk tower, you wouldn't even get your feet wet.

XV furniture, and the marble staircase with its ornately curlicued brass balustrade. Out back is a formal knot garden and coach house modeled on a Greek temple. ○ 1 hr. *Keizersgracht 672.* ☎ *020/624-5255. www.museumvanloon.nl. Admission 8€ adults, 6€ students, 4€ kids 6–18. Wed–Mon 11am–5pm. Closed Jan 1, Apr 27, and Dec 25. Tram: 16 or 24 to Keizersgracht.*

❹ ★★ **Centraal Station.** Jump on any of the trams heading north to Centraal Station, which is an architectural masterpiece in its own right. Designed by architect Pierre Cuypers, who also built the **Rijksmuseum** (see p 7), it was built between 1884 and 1889 on three artificial islands in the IJ channel. Amsterdammers thoroughly disliked it at the time, but now it is loved for its extravagant Dutch Revivalist facade. The left-hand central tower has a gilded weather vane; the right one has a clock. Canal cruises leave from here, and most major trams have stops outside. Take time to soak up the buzz that swirls around the station in a blur of people, backpacks, bikes, trams, buses, vendors, pickpockets, and junkies. ○ 20 min. *Tram: 16 or 26 to Centraal Station.*

❺ ★★★ **EYE Film Institute.** Take the free ferry crossing from behind at Centraal Station. The pristine white shape of Amsterdam's new film museum hovers over the north bank of the River IJ like a mantis. Built in 2012 by Austrian architects **Delugan Meissl Associated Architects**, the EYE is the first major public building to be constructed north of the river. Its gleaming complex houses four movie theaters, exhibitions, a store, and a restaurant with a sought-after terrace with views back to Centraal Station. Although there's an admission fee for the movies and temporary exhibitions, the 360-degree Panorama

The EYE building is a gateway to the world of the moving image.

Amsterdam's Gables

The landmark townhouses and warehouses of Amsterdam's old center all have gables and it is easy to judge their age by their shape. Simple triangular, wooden gables came first, and then spout gables (Keizersgracht 403) with a little point on top were used, mostly on warehouses, in the 14th century. These simply followed the pitch of the roof, but over time, more ornate designs crept in. Step gables were popular in the 17th century (Brouwersgracht 2 in the Jordaan), and elegant, straight neck gables (Herengracht 168) adorned with ornamental shoulders appeared between 1640 and 1780. Rounded bell-shaped gables (Prinsengracht 359) were introduced in the late 17th century and remained popular until the end of the 18th century.

The hook sitting central on most of these gables is called a *hijsbalk* and was used with a rope and pulley system for hauling cumbersome items in and out of houses with steep, narrow staircases. Most of the canalside houses lean a tad forward to prevent loads crashing into the facades.

Amsterdam has a range of historic gable styles.

film display in the basement is free to access. EYE is a cash-free zone. ⏱ *1 hr. IJpromenade 1.* ☎ *020/589-1400. www.eyefilm.nl. Admission movie: 10€ adults, 8.50€ students, 7.50€ kids 10 and under; exhibitions: 9€ adults, 7.50€ students, free for kids 10 and under. Sun–Thurs 10am–10pm; Fri–Sat 10am–11pm. Ferry: From Waterplein West dock behind Centraal Station to Buiksloterweg.*

🍷 ★★ EYE Bar-Restaurant.
Currently one of the hottest tickets in Amsterdam, with a suntrap terrace table being the hottest of all. Dinner here is expensive but a lighter snack menu is served during the day, offering salads, soups, and quiches. *IJpromenade 1.* ☎ *020/589-1402. http://eyebarrestaurant.nl. $$.*

7 ★★ Museum Het Schip.
Back at Centraal Station, take bus no. 22 west to the city's most famous example of Amsterdam School architecture. The movement's designs were influenced by the socialist ideals of Hendrik Berlage and are epitomized by heavy use of brickwork, elaborate masonry, spiky towers, painted glass, and wrought-iron work. Michel de Klerk (1884–1923) was the leading exponent of the school and designed his seminal building Het Schip to resemble an ocean liner; the brick complex incorporated social housing, a school, and a post office. The latter is the only one of De Klerk's interiors currently open to the public, but at press time, the school was being restored

Amsterdam's Addresses

The gables on Amsterdam houses were there for decoration and to hide the pitch of the roof but also had another function, which was to help identify the building before postal addresses were invented. To help this, *gevelstenen* (gable stones) of ornamental tiles, sculptures, or reliefs that played on the original owner's name or profession were added to the facades to make identification easier. Walls in the Begijnhof and on Sint-Luciënsteeg at the **Amsterdam Museum** (see p 12) have some pretty gable stones, including the oldest known, dating from 1603 and showing a milkmaid carrying her buckets. Then the French came along and annexed The Netherlands in 1806, introducing a system of house numbers to Amsterdam and spoiling all the fun.

for opening in late 2014. ① *30 min. Spaarndammerplantsoen 140.* ☎ *020/686-8595. www.hetschip. nl. Admission 7.50€ adults, 5€ students, free for kids 11 and under. Tues–Sun 11am–5pm. Closed Jan 1, Easter, Apr 27, and Dec 25. Bus: 22 to Zaanstraat.*

Museum Het Schip.

⑧ ★★★ Westergasfabriek. Walk back through the Westerpark to the latest cultural offering on Amsterdam's scene. This enormous construction was built in the late 19th century as a gas factory supplying the rail tracks nearby and now has been transformed into an edgy party-central. The redbrick edifice hides cinemas, bars, galleries, and classy restaurants and has given a new lease on life to the Westerpark. *Polonceaukade 27.* ☎ *020/586-0710. www.wester gasfabriek.nl.*

☕ ★ Het Ketelkeuken. Industrial chic hangout at the Westergasfabriek cinema serving organic cheeses and salamis, wheat beers, and frothy cappuccino. The clientele often includes Dutch movie actors. *Pazzanistraat 4.* ☎ *020/684-0090. www.ketelhuis.nl. $.*

Amsterdam with Kids

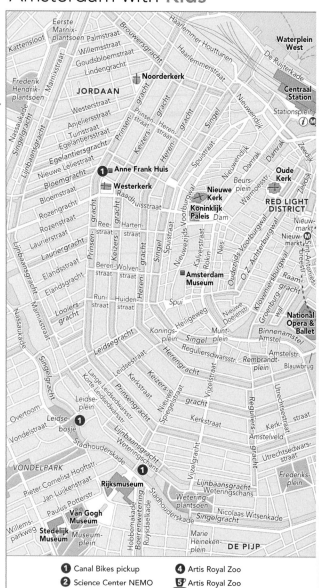

1 Canal Bikes pickup

2 Science Center NEMO

3 Hortus Botanicus

4 Artis Royal Zoo

5 Artis Royal Zoo

6 Tropenmuseum

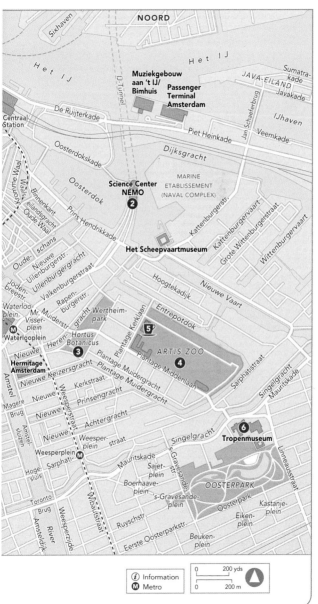

NOORD

Sixhaven

Het IJ

Het IJ

Sumatra-kade

JAVA-EILAND

Javakade

Muziekgebouw aan 't IJ/ Bimhuis

Passenger Terminal Amsterdam

IJ-Tunnel

De Ruijterkade

Jan Schaeferbrug

IJhaven

Veemkade

Centraal Station

Piet Heinkade

Oosterdokskade

Dijksgracht

Nieuwe Waal

Waals-eilandsgracht

Oude Waal

Oosterdok

Prins Hendrikkade

Binnenkant

Science Center NEMO
2

MARINE ETABLISSEMENT (NAVAL COMPLEX)

Kattenburgerstr.

Kattenburgervaart

Grote Wittenburgervaart

Wittenburgervaart

Het Scheepvaartmuseum

Oude schans

Nieuwe Uilenburgerstr.

Uilenburgergracht

Valkenburgerstraat

Rapen-burgerstr.

Hoogtekadijk

Nieuwe Vaart

Joden-breestr.

Waterloo-plein

Mr. Visser-plein

Heren-gracht

Wertheim-park

5

Entrepotdok

M Waterlooplein

Nieuwe

Hortus Botanicus
3

Plantage Kerklaan

ARTIS ZOO

4

Sarphatistraat

Hermitage Amsterdam

Nieuwe Keizersgracht

Plantage Muidergracht

Plantage Middenlaan

Singelgracht

Mauritskade

Magere Brug

Amstel-sluizen

Nieuwe Prinsengracht

Kerkstraat

Plantage Muidergracht

Nieuwe Weesperstraat

Achtergracht

Amstel

Nieuwe Weesper-straat

Singelgracht

Tropenmuseum
6

Weesperplein

M

Mauritskade

Hoge-sluis

Weesperplein

Sarphati-

Sajet-plein

's-Gravesande-str.

Linneausstraat

Toronto Brug

Weesperzijde

Boerhaave-plein

's-Gravesande-plein

OOSTERPARK

Amsteldijk

Wibautstraat

Ruyschstr.

Oosterpark

Eiken-plein

Kastanje-plein

River

Eerste Oosterparkstr.

Beuken-plein

i Information

M Metro

0   200 yds

0   200 m

Despite the obvious considerations, Amsterdam caters brilliantly for children. The city offers modern, interactive museums carefully designed to appeal to youngsters; canal trips; trams to ride; and bikes to hire. With playgrounds in all the parks, kids' shows in several theaters, and pancakes on almost every menu, there's always something to do when youngsters get fractious or it pours with rain. However, as anyone with toddlers will tell you, pushing baby strollers across all those cobbles ain't much fun. START: Tram 1, 2, 4, 5, 9, 13, 16, 17, or 24 to Centraal Station.

❶ ★★★ **Canal Cruises.** There are a multitude of canal cruises to choose from: sedate hour-long potters around the main sights with commentary; the hop-on, hop-off Canal Bus service that allows families to build their own sightseeing itineraries; or Canal Bikes, which are giant pedalos and can be hired on Leidseplein, outside the **Anne Frank Huis** (see p 11), or near the **Rijksmuseum** (see p 7). For a lunchtime treat, try the Pannenkoekenboot (Pancake Boat; ☎ 020/638-8817; www.pannenkoekenboot.nl) for unlimited servings of pancakes with sweet or savory fillings. ⏲ *1–2 hr.*

An interactive exhibit at the Science Center NEMO.

❷ ★★★ **Science Center NEMO.** Walk to Oosterdok across Oosterdokskade. More play station than museum, NEMO is the best place to head for with kids if it's a rainy day. This accessible, hands-on, interactive science center is housed in a magnificent pale green, ship-shaped building designed by Renzo Piano in 1997. Its aim is to introduce science and technology to kids in an understandable form. It's a great experience for kids 7 or older, and kids ages 4 to 6 can go through a "Shadow World" especially designed for expanding young minds. Through games, experiments, and demonstrations, kids learn how chain reactions work, search for ETs, blow a soap bubble large enough to stand inside, and much more. There's a lab for supervised experiments, displays on harnessing green energies, and even simple explanations of the Big Bang. Some of the displays on the higher floors are aimed at teenagers and raise the thorny issue of sex; there's always lots of adolescent sniggering around the peep shows. NEMO's broad, stepped, and sloping roof is an attraction in itself, a place to hang out, have a beer or catch the sun in summer, and take in the views. At the top, you are 30m (98 ft.) above the IJ waterway and have sweeping views

Farming Fun for Kids

Children can be amateur farmers for a day at **Geitenboerderij de Ridammerhoeve,** Nieuwe Meerlaan 4 (☎ 020/645-5034; www.geitenboerderij.nl; bus: 170 or 172 to the Amsterdamse Bos [forest]). They get to feed goats and lambs (along with chickens, a calf or two, and a few potbelly hogs); clean stables, coops, and pens; milk a goat; and bottle-feed baby animals. The farm is open Wednesday to Monday from 10am to 5pm; admission is free. At the tiny **Kinderboerderij de Dierencapel,** Bickersgracht 207 (☎ 020/420-6855; www.dedierencapel.nl; bus: 18, 21, or 22), an urban petting zoo in the Western Islands neighborhood, west of Centraal Station, you'll find endearing piglets, kids (of the goat species), lambs, chickens, ducks, and rabbits; there's a play area, too. The petting zoo is open Tuesday to Sunday from 9am to 5pm; admission is free. Equally entertaining is **Kinderboerderij de Pijp,** Lizzy Ansinghstraat 82 (☎ 020/664-8303; www.kinderboerderijdepijp.nl; tram: 12 or 26), a children's farm off Ferdinand Bolstraat in the De Pijp (the Pipe) urban district south of the center. Here, in addition to the animals mentioned above, kids can get close to donkeys, ponies, peacocks, and turkeys. The farm is open Monday to Friday from 11am to 5pm, and Saturday to Sunday from 1 to 5pm; admission is free.

over the Old Harbor and Eastern Dock, plus the **Muziekgebouw aan 't IJ** concert hall (see p 117) and the fast-appearing new architectural horizon around the River IJ. Snacks are served in Café DEK5, which has a grand outdoor terrace, and modest menus in Café Renzo Piano. ○ 2 hr. Oosterdok 2. ☎ 020/531-3233. www.e-nemo.nl. Admission 15€, free for kids 3 and under. Tues–Sun 10am–5:30pm. Closed Jan 1, Apr 27, and Dec 25. Bus: 22 or 48 to Kadijksplein.

❸ ★★ Hortus Botanicus (Botanical Garden). Walk back to Centraal Station and catch tram 9 or 14 to Muiderstraat for a treasure-trove of tropical plants, steamy hothouses, and exotic palm trees

brought back from former Dutch colonies across the world. These botanical gardens were established in 1682 and are packed with 115,000 rare plants and trees; in summer, the lovely landscape explodes with the colors and scents of more than 250,000 flowers. The three-climate greenhouse gets progressively warmer as you walk through it—most of the plants here come from Australia and South Africa. There's also an herb garden, a desert greenhouse, a tree-spotting route through the gardens, and a butterfly house with free-flying giant butterflies that kids love. ○ 1 hr. Plantage Middenlaan 2A. ☎ 020/625-9021. www.dehortus.nl. Admission 8.50€ adults; 4.50€ seniors, students, and kids 5–14.

Kids will love seeing the monkeys at the Artis Zoo.

Daily 10am–5pm. Closed Jan 1 and Dec 25. Tram: 9 or 14 to Muiderstraat.

❹ ★★ **Artis Royal Zoo.** Continue down Muiderstraat and turn left on to Plantage Kerklaan. Amsterdam's zoo was established in 1838 and covers more than 14 hectares (35 acres) of tree-lined pathways and landscaped gardens. It has more than 900 species of animals, combining a 19th-century ambience with a 21st-century emphasis on conservation and breeding. Buy a map and a list of the current feeding times from the Artis office at the zoo's entrance to negotiate the animal enclosures—where lions, leopards, elephants, giraffes, and gazelles range fairly freely. Admission is included to Artis's Aquarium, Insect House, Geological

Museum, and Planetarium for 3D films on the birth of the planet. There's also a children's farm, where kids can pet assorted small animals. There are daily keeper talks, vulture- and lion-feeding sessions, playful sea lions, and elephant training to fit in to your day as well, plus late-night sessions at the zoo on Saturdays between June and the end of August. ⏱ *3–5 hr. Plantage Kerklaan 38–40.* ☎ *0900/ 278-4796. www.artis.nl. Admission 20€ adults, 17€ kids 3–9; you can purchase tickets online. Nov–Feb daily 9am–5pm; Mar–Oct daily 9am– 6pm. Tram: 9 or 14 to Artis.*

❺ ★★ **Artis Royal Zoo.** There are six eating options at the zoo, from tray bikes selling waffles and sodas to casual self-service eateries with salads and waffles or a formal restaurant with views of the flamingo pond. *Plantage Kerklaan. $–$$.*

❻ ★★★ **Tropenmuseum.** Trams 9 and 14 both stop right outside the Tropenmuseum out in the boondocks of Oosterpark. Holland's Royal Institute for the Tropics owns this unusual museum devoted to the study of the cultures of tropical areas around the world. Breathing life into the sights, smells, and sounds of the tropics and subtropics, this superb anthropological museum originally took as its central

A sculpture from the Tropenmuseum.

Rainy Day Options

There's plenty more for families to do in Amsterdam when it's raining. The Anne Frank Huis (see p 11) will challenge and interest children aged 9 and up but can confuse younger kids, and it is not at all stroller friendly. Madame Tussauds on Dam Square (☎ 020/522-1010; www.madametussauds.com) is perennially popular with older kids for its waxwork models of Johnny Depp, Gwyneth Paltrow, and Ronaldhino, and now the new Dutch King Willem-Alexander and his family have joined them. The Amsterdam Dungeon (☎ 020/530-8500; www.thedungeons.com/amsterdam) may well terrify youngsters, but teens will adore it for the gory interpretations of the Spanish Inquisition and burning witches at the stake.

theme the role of The Netherlands as colonial power across the Far East, South America, and the Dutch Caribbean. Today, the displays go far beyond this colonial-era mindset to embrace contemporary issues such as the causes of poverty in the developing world and the depletion of the world's tropical rainforests. And they start them young: The Tropenmuseum Junior's new MixMax Brasil is an interactive display encouraging kids between 6 and 13 to understand different cultures. (Tropenmuseum Junior is open only Sat, Sun, and school holidays 11 am–5 pm. Admission is separate from the primary

Tropenmuseum: 12€ adults, 8€ kids 4–18.) Among the museum's collection of 250,000 artifacts, youngsters love the walk-through peasant house in Java, the Arab souk, the Mongolian yurt, and the elaborate wedding costumes from Thailand. The building itself is noteworthy for its ornamented 1920s facade bristling with turrets, step gables, arched windows, and delicate spires. ⏱ 2 hr. Linnaeusstraat 2. ☎ 020/568-8200. www.tropenmuseum.nl. Admission 13€ adults; 8€ seniors, students, and kids 4–17. Tues–Sun 10am–5pm. Closed Jan 1, Apr 27, and Dec 25. Tram: 3 or 7 to Linnaeusstraat.

Amsterdam & the IJ

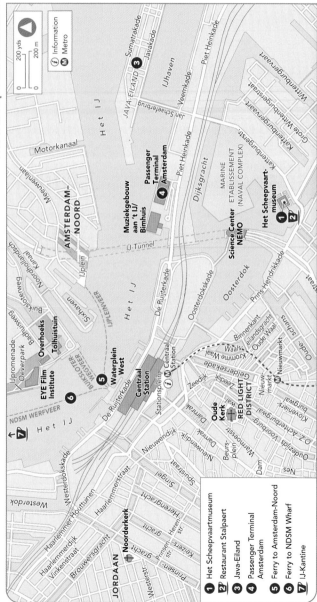

1 Het Scheepvaartmuseum
2 Restaurant Stalpaert
3 Java-Eiland
4 Passenger Terminal Amsterdam
5 Ferry to Amsterdam-Noord
6 Ferry to NDSM Wharf
7 IJ-Kantine

Holland's history and culture are inextricably linked with the sea, as you'll discover for yourself on a maritime exploration of Amsterdam. This tour takes you to one of the country's best maritime museums; guides you to a redeveloped, residential harbor island and an ultramodern cruise liner dock; and sails you around the shipping channel by ferry. You'll see the stylish new architecture of the Muziekgebouw aan 't IJ concert hall and the EYE Film Institute as well as other burgeoning new cultural centers across the River IJ in Amsterdam Noord, fast becoming the district to watch for the future. START: **Bus 22, 42, or 43 to Kattenburgerplein.**

Scheepvaartmuseum (Maritime Museum).

1 ★★ kids Het Scheepvaart-museum (National Maritime Museum). Housed in a mammoth, Venetian-style 17th-century arsenal, Amsterdam's Maritime Museum is a gem, completely remodeled and reopened in 2011. Its displays showcase the importance of Amsterdam's maritime history. There are many paintings and models of ships, seascapes, navigational instruments, and cannons and other weaponry scattered through the displays, which have been spruced up with the clever use of interactive light, sound, multimedia, and audiovisual aids. The best exhibitions detail the growth of the Dutch East India Company (V.O.C.) and sensitively address the slave trade and whaling issues. Special exhibits aimed at kids tell the story of lots of naval derring-do, but the main point of a trip to this museum is for youngsters to get on board the gaily painted, full-size replica of the V.O.C. merchant ship *Amsterdam*, moored on the quay outside. Everything on board is as it was in 1749 when the original boat

Java-Eiland and KNSM-Eiland are filled with modern residential buildings.

foundered on its maiden voyage to the East Indies (present-day Indonesia). Actors portraying sailors fire cannons, sing sea shanties, mop the deck, hoist cargo on board, and attend a solemn "burial at sea." Kids can join sail makers and rope makers at work and see the cook prepare a shipboard meal in the galley. ○ *3 hr. Kattenburgerplein 1.* ☎ *020/523-2222. www.het scheepvaartmuseum.nl. Admission 15€ adults, 7.50€ students and kids 5–17. Daily 9am–5pm. Bus: 22 or 48 to Kadijksplein.*

The Passenger Terminal Amsterdam.

2 ★ **Restaurant Stalpaert.** Catch your breath in the Maritime Museum's smartly kitted out and eco-friendly restaurant. You'll have great views over the Oosterdok as you tuck into Dutch cheese platters or healthy turkey salads. Kids have their own menu, which happily includes Ben & Jerry's ice cream. *Kattenburgerplein 1.* ☎ *020/523-2222. $.*

3 ★ **Java-Eiland.** Explore the recently redeveloped Entrepotdok and catch tram 10 on Sarphatistraat for the two man-made islands of Java and KNSM. These were once thickly strewn with dilapidated harbor warehouses and other port installations but have been amalgamated to form one long island. Wandering along the riverfront promenade of this shiny slice of modern residential zone gives an indication of where the growth of Amsterdam is headed in the 21st century. ○ *30 min. IJhaven. Tram: 10 to Azartplein.*

4 ★ **Passenger Terminal Amsterdam (PTA).** Cross Jan Schaeferbrug over the IJ to the ultramodern facility just east of Centraal Station. The PTA is best visited when a giant oceangoing cruise liner is tied up at the dock on the IJ ship channel; it sees 200,000 passengers through its doors annually and also doubles up as an events venue. The neighboring building on the wharf is the shiny glass concert hall **Muziekgebouw aan 't IJ** (see p 117); the Bimhuis jazz club is next door. ⏱ *30 min. Piet Heinkade 27.* ☎ *020/509-1000. www.pt amsterdam.nl. Open when a cruise ship is moored. Free admission. Tram: 26 to Passenger Terminal Amsterdam.*

⑤ ★★ Ferry to Amsterdam-Noord. Walk to Centraal Station and take the free 5-minute ride on the Buiksloterwegveer (Buiksloterweg Ferry) from the Waterplein West dock across to the north bank of the IJ. You'll get a bird's-eye view of the city's busy harbor traffic and the chance to explore the innovative architecture of **the EYE Film Institute** (see p 29) and maybe have lunch or see a movie there. Also, check out the Tolhuistuin (Tolhuisweg 5; ☎ *020/763-0650; www.tolhuistuin.nl),* a new cultural center with three auditoriums on the old Shell factory complex. ⏱ *90 min. Ferry: Buiksloterwegveer.*

⑥ ★★ kids NDSM-Werf (Wharf). Back behind Centraal Station, board the free NDSM-Werfveer (NDSM Wharf Ferry) to the NDSM Wharf. This former dry dock

belonged to the Nederlandsche Dok en Scheepsbouw Maatschappij (Netherlands Dock and Shipyard Corporation) and was long derelict before being taken over by an artists' community known as Stichting Kinetisch Noord. Among the recycled street sculpture and heavy-duty graffiti, studios, galleries, and a theater have sprung up. This cutting-edge cultural center is growing in reputation as the **Westergasfabriek** (see p 31) becomes more mainstream. Here, too, is the **Amstel Botel** (see p 126), the city's only floating hotel. The elegant old triple-masted schooner *Pollux* is moored up alongside, and Greenpeace's retired environmental warrior of the seas, *Sirius,* is berthed across the dock from the Botel. The **Pannenkoekenboot** (see p 34) sorties from here to prowl the harbor laden with pancake-munching kids. ⏱ *1 hr. Ferry: NDSM-Werfveer.*

⑦ ★★★ IJ-Kantine. This cheery restaurant-cum-cafe on the NDSM Wharf is found in the industrial-chic former dockworkers' canteen. It serves food all day and has great waterfront views of the maritime activity on the IJ. *MT Ondinaweg 15–17.* ☎ *020/633-7162. www. ijkantine.nl. $$.*

The free NDSM Wharf Ferry.

Alternative Amsterdam

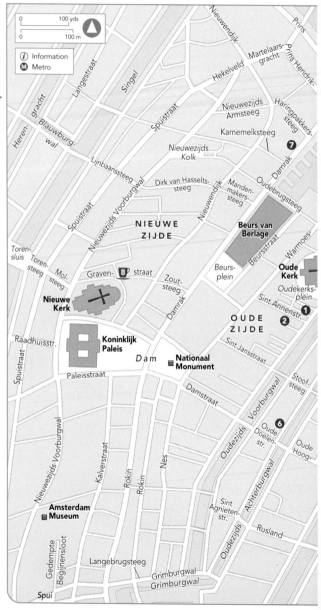

0   100 yds
0   100 m

ⓘ Information
Ⓜ Metro

Nieuwendijk

Martelaars-gracht

Prins

Prins Hendrik-

Langestraat

Singel

Hekelveld

Nieuwezijds
Armsteeg

Haringpakkers-
steeg

Heren-
gracht

Blauwburg-
wal

Spuistraat

Karnemelksteeg

❼

Lijnbaansteeg

Nieuwezijds
Kolk

Damrak

Spuistraat

Nieuwezijds Voorburgwal

Dirk van Hasselts-
steeg

Nieuwendijk

Manden-
makers-
steeg

Oudebrugsteeg

NIEUWE
ZIJDE

Beurs van
Berlage

Toren-
sluis

Toren-
steeg

Mol-
steeg

Graven- ❽ straat

Zout-
steeg

Beurs-
plein

Beursstraat

Warmoes

Oude
Kerk

Nieuwe
Kerk

Damrak

Oudekerks-
plein

❶

OUDE
ZIJDE

Sint Annenstr.

❷

Raadhuisstr.

Koninklijk
Paleis

Dam

Nationaal
Monument

Sint Jansstraat

Spuistraat

Paleisstraat

Damstraat

Oudezijds Voorburgwal

Oude
Doelen-
str.

Stoof-
steeg

❻

Oude
Hoog-

Nieuwezijds Voorburgwal

Kalverstraat

Nes

Rokin

Rokin

Sint
Agnieten-
str.

Oudezijds

Achterburgwal

Amsterdam
Museum

Rusland

Gedempte
Beginensloot

Langebrugsteeg

Grimburgwal

Grimburgwal

Spui

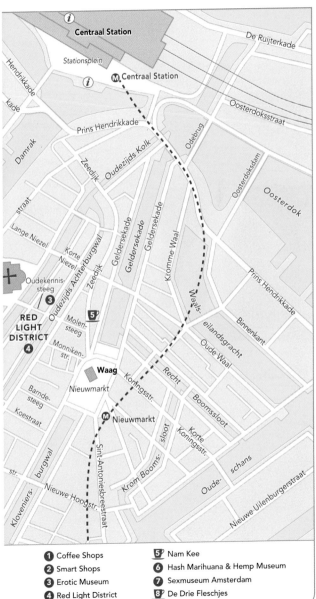

1 Coffee Shops
2 Smart Shops
3 Erotic Museum
4 Red Light District
5 Nam Kee
6 Hash Marihuana & Hemp Museum
7 Sexmuseum Amsterdam
8 De Drie Fleschjes

Amsterdam deservedly has a reputation for being a wild party town; prostitution and soft drugs are legal, and the city holds tolerant attitudes toward many aspects of life. It's multicultural and has been for centuries. But Amsterdam has always had its gritty substrata, originating with 17th-century sailors who scrambled off ships into the arms of prostitutes in the Red Light District. This walking tour explores the darker side of Amsterdam and helps you to navigate it safely. START: **Metro to Nieuwmarkt.**

An exhibit from the Erotic Museum.

❶ ★ **Coffee Shops.** Amsterdam's notorious coffee shops are not known for their *mochaccinos* but for selling marijuana and hashish. They have brought millions of euros into the city through cannabis tourism since the decriminalizing of soft drugs in 1976. Today, despite attempts to shut some down, more than 200 remain, mostly around the Red Light District. Currently operating under a legal gray cloud, they cannot advertise, sell alcohol, or sell drugs to anyone under age 18. It's illegal to buy drugs on the street in Amsterdam, so if you want a smoke, drop by a coffee shop where, ironically, nicotine is banned. The Bulldog at Oudezijds Voorburgwal 88 is the best known.

❷ ★★ **Smart Shops.** If you want to get high without smoking a joint or eating a space cake made with hashish, explore Amsterdam's smart shops, which sell natural stimulants such as *guarana* and supposed aphrodisiacs such as ginkgo biloba as well as magic mushrooms, growing kits for weed, *and seeds. Check out* Nightlife (Nieuwendijk 42) the Magic Mushroom Gallery (Spuistraat 249), or Azarius on Kerkstraat behind the Leidseplein.

❸ ★ **Erotic Museum.** Marginally less sexy than the (unsexy) Sexmuseum (below), this weak homage to erotica is spread over five floors, with one floor entirely dedicated to S&M (photo op here complete with handcuffs and whips). Otherwise, there are tons of rude antique figurines, some sketches by John Lennon, and a flea-bitten re-creation of a red-light window. A new addition is the Sexy Art Gallery, which shows and sells provocative soft-porn drawings and paintings. ⏱ *45 min. Oudezijds Achterburgwal 54.* ☎ *020/627-8954. www.erotisch-museum.nl. Admission 7€. Sun–Thurs 11am–1am, Fri–Sat 11am–2am. Tram: 4, 9, 16, or 24 to the Dam.*

❹ ★★ **Red Light District.** Upon leaving the Erotic Museum, you're in Amsterdam's infamous *Rosse Buurt* (Red Light District). If you take a peek down any of the tiny alleyways, you'll see the prostitutes hanging out behind their windows, posing and hoping to draw in customers. Many are in various

Cleaning Up the Red Light District

Amsterdam's Red Light District is notorious the world over for its "anything goes" vibe, but recently the warren of streets, also known as *Rosse Buurt*, *De Wallen*, or *De Walletjes*, has been undergoing a gentrification. Several of the city's infamous coffee shops and around half the brothel windows have been closed; at press time, the city fathers were halfway through a decade-long plan to sanitize the area and more closures will follow.

In the Red Light District, you'll find sex shops, live sex shows, and prostitutes waiting for customers behind windows.

the red lights reflecting off the canals. ⏱ *30 min. Along Oudezijds Achterburgwal and the tiny alleyways that intersect it. Metro: Nieuwmarkt.*

5 ☕ ★★★ **Nam Kee.** The most famous restaurant in Amsterdam's Chinatown is also one of its best; this family-run venue looks like nothing from the outside but the interior is full of life as plates of noodles, Peking duck, and beef spare ribs dripping in honey fly out of the kitchen. *Zeedijk 111–113.* ☎ *020/ 624-3470. www.namkee.net. $$.*

A display from the Hash Marihuana & Hemp Museum.

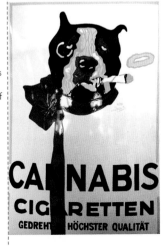

states of undress and currently most of the girls seem to be from Eastern Europe. If the curtains are closed, then you know that a deal is being consummated. What you'll notice most of all are the throngs of testosterone-driven men circling these tiny alleyways and egging each other on. Despite this, the Red Light District is seedy rather than dangerous, although keep an eye out for pickpockets and don't take pictures of the girls. Overall, the area is very well policed. Early evening is the best time to visit, before it gets crowded with drunks but late enough that you can see

A display from the Sexmuseum Amsterdam.

⑥ ★★ Hash Marihuana & Hemp Museum.

Along one of the Red Light District's main drags, this museum was reworked and reopened in 2012; it's not a bad place to start for anyone curious about the history of soft drugs and modern-day medicinal applications of hemp. The use of drugs is not promoted, nor can you buy drugs here. There's the predictable display of pipes—some beautifully carved—and bongs, some lovely old paintings depicting 16th-century farmers smoking dope, and lots of items made out of hemp. ⏱ 1 hr. Oudezijds Achterburgwal 148. ☎ 020/624-8926. www.hashmuseum.com. Admission 9€ adults, free for kids under 13 (must be accompanied by an adult). Daily 10am–10pm. Closed Apr 27. Tram: 4, 9, 16, or 24 to the Dam.

⑦ ★ Sexmuseum Amsterdam.

Walk up Damstraat to Amsterdam's "Venustempel," which opened in 1985 and is the oldest sex museum in the world. On the outskirts of the Red Light District, it attracts more than half a million visitors per year, wandering in a bemused manner around the muddled layouts, bumping into each other up and down stairs in two medieval houses that have been grafted together. There's not much about the history of sex here, just lots of erotic ephemera such as Chinese and Japanese figurines in compromising positions, waxwork figures in various states of undress and decay, and a rather random diorama of Marilyn Monroe in the famous scene from *The Seven Year Itch* in which her skirt is blown up by a subway vent. The most interesting display is of early erotic photography, around which red-faced teenagers stand giggling. ⏱ 1 hr. Damrak 18. ☎ 020/622-8376. www. sexmuseumamsterdam.com. Admission 4€; under 16 not admitted. Daily 9:30am–11:30pm. Closed Dec 25. Tram: 1, 2, 4, 5, 9, 13, 16, 17, 24, or 26 to Centraal Station.

⑧ ★★★ De Drie Fleschjes.

Sample some *jenever* (Dutch gin) in wholesome, old-fashioned surroundings. There's sawdust on the floor and barrels of *jenever* in this traditional *proeflakaal* (tasting room). Gravenstraat 18. ☎ 020/624-8443. www.dedriefleschjes.nl. $. ●

Amsterdam's Alternative Red Light Districts

Although Amsterdam's most famous Red Light District is around the Oude Kerk, there are two others. Singelgebied is bounded by the Nieuwezijds Voorburgwal and Singel canal; a few of the prostitutes here are transsexuals and there are gay sex shops and cinemas. The city's smallest Red Light district is south of the city center in De Pijp, on Ruysdaelkade along the Boerenwetering canal.

The Best Neighborhood Walks

The Old Center

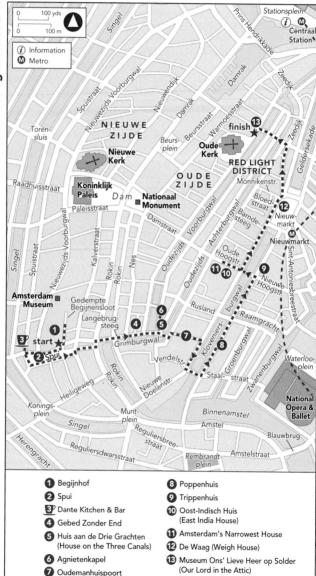

0   100 yds
0   100 m

ⓘ Information
Ⓜ Metro

❶ Begijnhof
❷ Spui
❸🍴 Dante Kitchen & Bar
❹ Gebed Zonder End
❺ Huis aan de Drie Grachten (House on the Three Canals)
❻ Agnietenkapel
❼ Oudemanhuispoort
❽ Poppenhuis
❾ Trippenhuis
❿ Oost-Indisch Huis (East India House)
⓫ Amsterdam's Narrowest House
⓬ De Waag (Weigh House)
⓭ Museum Ons' Lieve Heer op Solder (Our Lord in the Attic)

Previous page: Biking in the Jordaan neighborhood.

T̲ake a stroll through the medieval core of old Amsterdam, the epicenter from which the city expanded outwards in the 1660s. Here you'll find the oldest and narrowest houses, ornately decorated facades, and one or two surprises in a confusing tangle of narrow streets that's a world away from the gridlike regularity of the Grachtengordel (Canal Ring). START: **Tram 1, 2, 4, 5, 9, 14, 16, or 24 to Spui.**

The Begijnhof garden.

❶ ★★ **Begijnhof.** Entered through an ornate gate off Spui, this cluster of photogenic gabled houses around a leafy garden courtyard is the perfect place to feel the ambience of old Amsterdam. Black-painted no. 34 is the city's oldest house, built around 1455, and is one of only two timber houses remaining in the city. Amsterdam was a destination for religious pilgrims and an important Catholic center before the Calvinist rebellion and Alteration in 1578. The Begijnhof was a *hofje* (almshouse, see p 50) built to offer devout women (*beguines*) the option to live independently of husband and children, and without becoming a nun, at a time when such a thing was unheard of. The *hofje* remained in operation for centuries after the changeover of the city from Catholicism to Protestantism and the last *beguine* died in 1971 at the age of 84. The Engelse Kerk (English Church) dates to 1607 and is used today by British ex-pats. Opposite the church, at no. 30, is the Begijnhofkapel, a secret Catholic chapel

dating from 1671 that's also still in use today. The Begijnhof is now a residence for seniors. ◷ *30 min. Spui and Gedempte Begijnensloot. No phone. Free admission. Daily 9am–5pm.*

❷ ★ **Spui.** Back into noisy reality, this square (pronounced *spow*) is both elegant and animated. At its south end is a statue of a small boy, *Het Lieverdje (The Little Darling)*, who is supposed to represent a typically mischievous Amsterdam child. Across the street, at no. 21, is the Maagdenhuis, the main

Spui.

downtown building of the University of Amsterdam.

3 ★ **Dante Kitchen & Bar.** With a brasserie-style wooden interior and an open kitchen, Dante's deals in simple food stylishly delivered: pizza, pasta, *bitterballen*, and delicious fries in mayo. The vast wooden bar displays more than 900 bottles of wines, spirits, and beers. *Spuistraat 320.* ☎ *020/774-7473. www.amsterdamdante.com. $$.*

4 ★ **Gebed Zonder End.** *Go to the east end of Spui, cross Rokin and Nes, and walk along Langebrugsteeg to Grimburgwal.* The tiny, flower-filled alleyway of Gebed Zonder End is located in an area between Nes and Oudezijds Voorburgwal that boasted more than 20 monasteries and convents in medieval times. Legend has it that you could always hear the murmur of prayers from behind the walls. Today, however, you're much more likely to hear laughter and chatter coming from the restaurant Kapitein Zeppos (see p 96).

The redbrick House on the Three Canals.

5 ★ **Huis aan de Drie Grachten (House on the Three Canals).** Continue along Grimburgwal, then cross Oudezijds Voorburgwal and Oudezijds Achterburgwal. Between these two waterways and abutting Grimburgwal canal, you'll spot the handsomely restored, redbrick and step-gabled Dutch Renaissance mansion built in 1609, with red-painted wooden shutters. In the

Amsterdam's Hofjes

Amsterdam has many secret courtyards surrounded by alms-houses—they could be considered an early form of care in the community where the poor or disadvantaged of the parish could be housed and supported. The best known is the Begijnhof (see p 49), where a community of pious women lived for several centuries. The Hermitage Amsterdam is also housed in a former *hofje*, where homes were provided for elderly women of slender means. Zon's Hofje at Prinsengracht 159–171 is another example; the outer door is open between 10am and 5pm Monday through Saturday, and you can walk quietly through the passageway to the serene courtyard. A walk around the pretty streets of the Jordaan will reveal several *hofjes*, such as the Raepenhofje (see p 60) and the Suyckerhofje (see p 59).

early 20th century, this was a bookstore that used to print clandestine literature during World War II. *Oudezijds Voorburgwal 249.*

❻ ★ Agnietenkapel. Stroll a short way along Oudezijds Voorburgwal to no. 229–231, where you'll spot an elaborately ornamental gateway from 1571. This leads to the chapel (1470) of what was the St. Agnes Convent until the Protestant takeover of Amsterdam in 1578. It later became part of the Athenaeum Illustre, the city's first university, which was formed in 1632, and today houses a university conference center. *Oudezijds Voorburgwal 229–231.*

❼ ★★ Oudemanhuispoort. Backtrack to the House on the Three Canals and cross the bridge to the far side of Oudezijds Achterburgwal. Pass the Gasthuis, once a hospital and now part of the university campus, and turn right into a dimly lit arcade, the Oudemanhuispoort, which hosts a book market Monday to Saturday 9am to 5pm. Further down the passageway on the left, you'll see a doorway leading to a courtyard garden featuring a bust of Minerva, placed there in 1881. It's a lovely spot for a few minutes of solitude. *Off Grimburgwal.*

❽ ★ Poppenhuis. Turn right on Kloveniersburgwal and cross over the canal on Staalstraat; turn left

until you reach this handsome classical mansion built in 1642 by the highly successful architect Philips Vingboons for Joan Poppen, the dissolute son and heir to Jacob Poppen, a rich merchant who was a three-time mayor of Amsterdam. *Kloveniersburgwal 95.*

❾ ★ Trippenhuis. Nearby you'll see a double-fronted house built between 1660 and 1664 by Jacob Vingboons, the sibling of Philips, for the Trip brothers, who were arms dealers. This explains the martial images and emblems dotted about the house. Originally there were two houses behind a single classical facade, but they have since been joined and now house the Royal Netherlands Academy of Arts and Sciences. The building is not open for visitors. *Kloveniersburgwal 29.*

❿ ★★ Oost-Indisch Huis (East India House). Walk back to Bushuissluis canal bridge and cross over to Oude Hoogstraat, where you can enter this impressive 1606 building via a courtyard on the left side of the street. Once the warehouses and headquarters of the Vereenigde Oostindische Compagnie, or V.O.C. (Dutch East India Company), ship crews were recruited here and the company's invaluable collections of primitive maps were stored here. The house

Oost-Indisch Huis (East India House).

Amsterdam's narrowest house.

now belongs to the university. It's not officially open for visits, but you can stroll into the courtyard and through the doors to take a peek at the hallways hung with paintings of the 17th-century Dutch trading settlement of Batavia (now Jakarta, Indonesia). *Oude Hoogstraat 24.*

⓫ ★ **Amsterdam's Narrowest House.** In stark contrast to the gigantic facade of East India House, next door is the city's teeniest house. Squashed in next to Hendrik de Keyser's ornate church gate, Oude Hoogstraat 22 is just 2m (6½ ft.) wide and was built around 1733 as a single story; this miniscule abode was rented out to a watchmaker, and by 1787, etchings show that it had gained two more floors and a bell gable. Blink and you'll miss it. Head back to Kloveniersburgwal and go left. At nos. 10–12 is the drugstore Jacob Hooy & Co., which has been dispensing medicinal relief since 1743. *Oude Hoogstraat 22.*

⓬ ★★ **De Waag (Weigh House).** Kloveniersburgwal ends at Nieuwmarkt, a large and buzzing piazza dominated by the massive edifice that was once one of the city's medieval gates. The Waag later became the city's weigh house for goods coming in off the ships (see p 28) and now it's a great place to loiter over a cocktail to watch Amsterdam at play. Nieuwmarkt itself is the gateway to both the Red Light District and Chinatown. *Nieuwmarkt.*

⓭ ★★ **Museum Ons' Lieve Heer op Solder (Our Lord in the Attic).** To wind up your exploration of Amsterdam's old heart, stroll down Zeedijk, cross over the canal to Oudezijds Voorburgwal and discover one of the city's best-kept historical secrets. Following the Alteration and the sacking of all the churches in 1578, practicing Roman Catholicism was banned, so the Catholics had to find ways to worship in secret. Between 1661 and 1663, the wealthy Catholic merchant Jan Hartman bought this house and two others behind it and converted all three attics into a clandestine but lushly decorated Catholic chapel. Worshipers entered from a side street and climbed the narrow stairs to the hidden third-floor church, which could accommodate a congregation of 150. The secret chapel was recently renovated, its splendid Baroque flourishes, organ, marble columns, and oil paintings behind the altar once more shining like new. A new visitor center is being built in the adjoining house and rooms decorated in period style are opening up on the lower floors to enhance the museum. ⏱ *1 hr. Oudezijds Voorburgwal 40.* ☎ *020/624-6604. www.opsolder.nl. Admission 8€ adults, 4€ students and kids 6–18. Mon–Sat 10am–5pm, Sun and holidays 1–5pm. Closed Apr 27. Metro: Nieuwmarkt.*

Amsterdam's **Canal Ring**

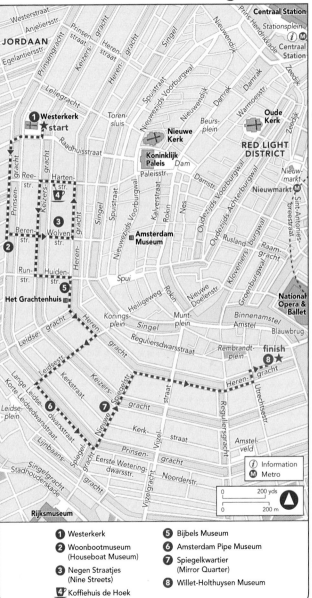

1. Westerkerk
2. Woonbootmuseum (Houseboat Museum)
3. Negen Straatjes (Nine Streets)
4. ☕ Koffiehuis de Hoek
5. Bijbels Museum
6. Amsterdam Pipe Museum
7. Spiegelkwartier (Mirror Quarter)
8. Willet-Holthuysen Museum

Amsterdam's glory days date back to the 17th century, an era rightly known as the Golden Age, and there's nowhere better to see the awesome architecture of that time than on the UNESCO-listed Grachtengordel (Canal Ring), which was built as the city expanded outwards in a grid pattern, adding three extra canals: Herengracht (Gentlemens' Canal), Keizersgracht (Emperor's Canal), and Prinsengracht (Princes' Canal). The diversity of styles is thanks to the wealthy buyers designing their houses to individual tastes; today this is an area of majestic mansions strung along tranquil canals. START: **Tram 3, 14, or 17 to Westerkerk.**

Canal houses in Amsterdam.

1 ★ Westerkerk. Just round the corner from the Anne Frank Huis, the Protestant Westerkerk is yet another ecclesiastical masterpiece by the celeb architect of the time, Hendrick de Keyser, who designed the Noorderkerk and the Zuiderkerk as part of the new development of the Grachtengordel (Canal Ring). The foundation stone was laid in 1620 (De Keyser died a year later), and the tower was finally completed in 1638; it is more than 85m (279 ft.) tall and is topped with the Crown

of Maximilian. Every 15 minutes, the tinkly carillon bells ring out across the city. The church itself is austere; in chime with the Calvinist beliefs of the time, there is no altar but the gold and silver pipes and Baroque sculpture adorning the organ make up for the lack of ornamentation. It is the burial place of Rembrandt—although no one knows where his grave is on the unmarked stone floor—and the venue for several royal weddings. ⏱ 30 min. Prinsengracht 281. ☎ 020/624-7766. www.westerkerk. nl. Free admission; 4€ for Westerpass guide. Mon–Sat 10am–3pm, Sun services only.

2 ★ Woonbootmuseum (Houseboat Museum). Two blocks down Prinsengracht to the left is a glimpse into the life of Amsterdam's 2,500 houseboat residents. The Houseboat Museum is found on board the *Hendrika Maria*, a former freighter built in 1914. A tour reveals the surprisingly roomy timber-roofed living space with box beds, a couple of armchairs, and a tiny cafe. ⏱ 15 min. Prinsengracht 296K. ☎ 020/427-0750. www.houseboatmuseum.nl. Admission 4€ adults, 3€ kids 5–15. Daily 11am–5pm. Closed Jan 1, 2 weeks in Jan, Apr 27, Dec 25–26, and Dec 31.

An exhibit from the Bijbels Museum (Biblical Museum).

❸ ★★ Negen Straatjes (Nine Streets). Turn down Berenstraat into one of Amsterdam's funky shopping areas, consisting of nine side streets running between Herengracht and Prinsengracht, a one-stop shopping destination with 36 chic stores selling high-end clothing from independent designers, artisan jewelry, organic soaps, and vintage fashions, all interspersed with plenty of bars, restaurants, and boutique hotels. The smart Pulitzer Hotel (see p 132) is just a step away. ⏱ *1 hr. Between Herengracht and Prinsengracht. www.the ninestreets.com. Most stores open Mon 1–5pm and Tues–Sun 10am–5pm.*

❹ ★★ Koffiehuis de Hoek. An old-style Amsterdam cafe on the corner overlooking the canal, this place positively bursts at the seams at lunchtime. Grab a table for an all-day breakfast or join the take-away line for sandwiches piled high with salami and salad. *Prinsengracht 341.* ☎ *020/625-3872. www. koffiehuisamsterdam.nl. $.*

❺ ★ Bijbels Museum. Just south of the Nine Streets on Herengracht are majestic vistas of vast mansions with their varied gables. Two of a group of four 1660s houses (nos. 364–370) with delicate neck gables contain the Biblical Museum. The houses are notable for being designed by architect Philips Vingboons for timber merchant Jacob Cromhout, but the museum itself is nothing to write home about. It suffers from a ramshackle layout and the few exhibits are odd in the extreme: a model of the temple in Jerusalem, some religious tapestries, and a few dusty bibles in a little room on the extravagantly carved wooden staircase. Two floors are under renovation and there's just not that much to see. However, the house itself is beautiful so be sure to check that out. ⏱ *20 min. Herengracht 366–368.* ☎ *020/624-2436. www.bijbels museum.nl. Admission 8€ adults, 6€ students, 4€ kids 5–18. Tues–Sat 10am–5pm; Sun and holidays 11am–5pm. Closed Jan 1 and Apr 27.*

❻ ★★ Amsterdam Pipe Museum. Continue down the block and if you haven't already been, go to **Het Grachtenhuis** (the Canal Museum; see p 8) to learn about the expansion of Amsterdam's canals in a truly engaging museum. Walk one block further and turn right down Leidsestraat, crossing over Prinsengracht, and turning left along its south side to the Amsterdam Pipe Museum. Although this may appear to be a niche market, in fact this display of pipes and its eccentric owner are quite entrancing. The curiously old-fashioned Smokiana shop is in the basement, selling pipes and books about pipes. Go up the steps to the museum and you'll be treated

The Best Neighborhood Walks

A period room from the Museum Willet-Holthuysen.

to a guided tour of the world's largest collection of Dutch clay pipes, intricately carved and bejeweled Meerschaum pipes, and bronze cast pipes from Cameroon. You'll also get to drink in the rarified atmosphere of the traditional 17th-century house renovated in 19th-century fashion. ① *45 min. Prinsengracht 488.* ☎ *020/421-1779. www.pijpenkabinet.nl. Admission 8€ adults, 4€ kids 17 and under. Wed–Sat noon–6pm. Closed Jan 1, Apr 27, and Dec 25.*

⑦ ★★ Spiegelkwartier (Mirror Quarter). Continue along Prinsengracht and turn left up Nieuwe Spiegelstraat to Kerkstraat on the canal bend; this has been Amsterdam's main

antiques-dealing center for nearly 100 years. This posh little locale has more than 100 stores selling paintings, antiques, Russian icons, silver, gold jewelry, and of course, plenty of genuine blue-and-white Delft-ware. From here it's an easy hop over the Singel to the **Rijksmuseum** (see p 7) or turn right along Vijzelstraat until you hit Herengracht once more and take a right. ① *30 min. Spiegelgracht.* ☎ *020/ 623-4748. www.spiegelkwartier.nl. Shop hours vary but roughly Tues–Sat 11am–5pm.*

⑧ ★★★ Willet-Holthuysen Museum. On the left side of the Herengracht is a magical museum with a pristine interior dating from the 19th century. This perfectly restored canal house shouts money; it's redolent of the sybaritic lifestyle of Amsterdam's prosperous merchant classes, and every curtain, every piece of furniture displayed, and every choice of wallpaper, down to the deep-blue fabric in the gentleman's parlor, is in keeping with the period. Displays include an introduction to the aristocratic family who lived here and a collection of painstakingly detailed silver figurines. There's an exquisite formal knot garden at the rear of the house. ① *1 hr. Herengracht 605.* ☎ *020/523-1822. www.willet holthuysen.nl. Admission 8€ adults, 6€ students, 4€ kids 5–18. Mon–Fri 10am–5pm, Sat–Sun and public holidays 11am–5pm. Closed Apr 27 and Dec 25.*

The Jordaan

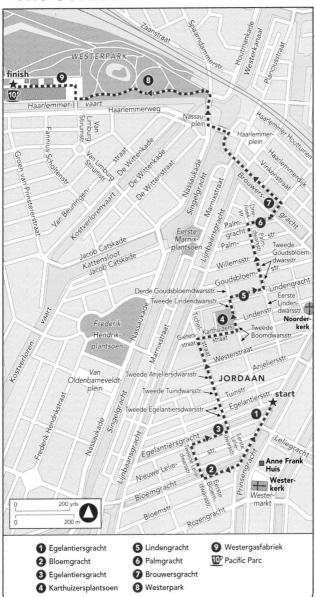

1 Egelantiersgracht
2 Bloemgracht
3 Egelantiersgracht
4 Karthuizersplantsoen
5 Lindengracht
6 Palmgracht
7 Brouwersgracht
8 Westerpark
9 Westergasfabriek
10 Pacific Parc

The Jordaan is one of Amsterdam's loveliest and most distinctive neighborhoods, once the province of the working classes but now thoroughly gentrified and home to many of the city's intelligentsia. Among the district's charms are narrow streets, tiny canals crossed with humpbacked bridges, and several delightful, centuries-old almshouses, or *hofjes* (see p 50), as well as on-trend galleries, traditional brown cafes (see p 108), and bars. Aim for mid-afternoon when you start this walk, and you'll wind up in Westerpark in time for a beer in early evening. **START: Tram 3, 14, or 17 to Westerkerk.)**

Bloemgracht.

❶ ★ Egelantiersgracht. Start your walk outside the hardware store Gunters & Meuser at nos. 2–6, on the corner of Prinsengracht, for a fine example of Amsterdam School architecture, designed in 1917. Its intricate brickwork and cast-iron ornaments were influenced by the Art Nouveau style. To the left of the store, at no. 8, a step-gabled house dating from 1649 is decorated with sandstone ornaments and gable stones that depict the English monk St. Willibrord (the first bishop of Utrecht, in 695) and a brewer. *Prinsengracht 2–6.*

❷ ★ Bloemgracht. Turn right and walk along Prinsengracht

before taking a right onto Bloemgracht, the grandest of the Jordaan canals. Bloemgracht was originally home to workers who produced dyes and paints. Nos. 77 and 81 are former sugar refineries from 1752 and 1763, respectively. The three fine step-gabled houses at nos. 87–91 date from 1642, and are now owned by the Hendrick de Keyser Foundation, an organization that preserves buildings of architectural and historic importance throughout The Netherlands. Their carved gable stones represent a townsman, a countryman, and a seaman. *Bloemgracht 87–91.*

❸ ★★ Egelantiersgracht. Turn right on to Derde Leliedwarsstraat to reach Egelantiersgracht and bear right along the canal. Named for the eglantine rose or sweetbrier,

Egelantiersgracht.

An outdoor cafe on Lindengracht.

Egelantiersgracht is one of the city's most picturesque and tranquil small canals and is lined with 17th- and 18th-century houses. If the door is open, take a peek into the Andrieshofje at nos. 105–141. Cattle farmer Ivo Gerrittsszoon financed this almshouse of 36 houses, which was completed in 1617 and remodeled in 1884. A corridor decorated with Delft blue tiles leads up to a small courtyard with a manicured garden. *Egelantiersgracht 105–141.*

❹ ★★ Karthuizersplantsoen. From Egelantiersgracht, turn left onto Derde Egelantiersdwarsstraat, walk 2 blocks and take a right down Tuinstraat before turning on to Tweede Tuindwarsstraat. Carry on across Westerstraat and walk along Tichelstraat until you hit Karthuizersstraat. On this street at nos. 13–19 is a row of neck-gabled houses from 1737, named after the four seasons. At nos. 69–191, you'll find the Huyszitten-Weduwenhof, which dates from 1650 and used to shelter poor widows. Today students live in these houses, which surround a large interior courtyard. Nothing is left of the Carthusian monastery (1394) that once stretched from Karthuizersplantsoen to Lijnbaansgracht and was destroyed in the 1570s during the Alteration. A playground marks the spot where its cemetery stood. *Karthuizersstraat 13–19.*

❺ ★★ Lindengracht. Turn left onto Tweede Lindendwarsstraat to reach Lindengracht, and take a right down this street, which was once the Jordaan's most important canal—since filled in. It is now the scene of a lively Saturday street market. The 15 small houses (originally there were 19) of the pretty Suyckerhofje at Lindengracht 149–163 were built in 1667 as a refuge for Protestant widows of a "tranquil character," who had been abandoned by their husbands. The door may be closed but you can generally open it during daylight hours and walk along the narrow entrance corridor to a courtyard garden filled with flowers and plants. *Lindengracht 149–163.*

The Best Neighborhood Walks

Palmgracht.

6 ★ Palmgracht. Walk down to Tweede Goudsbloemdwarsstraat and carry on over Goudsbloem-straat and Willemsstraat until you reach Palmgracht. Turn right onto this tree-shaded street, which was once a canal. The house at nos. 28–38 hides a small cobblestone courtyard garden behind an orange door that's the entrance to the Raepenhofje, an almshouse from 1648. If you're lucky, the door will be open and you can peek into the courtyard. *Palmgracht 28–38.*

7 ★★ Brouwersgracht. Take a right and stroll leftwards along this enchanting old canal lined with houseboats and narrow, gabled facades that tilt discernibly for-wards. When you reach Haarlem-merplein on the edge of the Jordaan, cross over the Singel and follow noisy Houtmankade into the peace of Westerpark.

8 ★ Westerpark. Until the early 2000s, the Westerpark was a tiny patch of green in the otherwise grimy industrial wasteland around the gas works that lay to its west. Since then, new life has been breathed into the Westergasfab-riek, and the Westerpark has been extended and remodeled to

include open lawns and shady trees, tennis courts, skate parks, and play areas for kids. Summer sees plenty of free open-air con-certs here, and there's often a fair for kids.

9 ★★★ Westergasfabriek. Central to the Westerpark is this mammoth former gasworks, which became redundant with the advent of North Sea gas in the 1960s and fell into disrepair. It was saved from demolition by squatters who moved in and refused to move out again, and by 2003 the building had been repurposed into one of Amsterdam's coolest entertainment venues (see p 109), with plenty of chances for a beer or a coffee as well as exhibition spaces, design studios, and the **Het Ketelhuis** movie theater. *Polonceaukade 27.*

10 ★★ Pacific Parc. This venue is a trendy cafe by day, a brasserie by night, and a dance club that gets crammed at the weekend. In summer there's a terrace for dining outside and live folksy music. *Polon-ceaukade 23, Westergasfabriek.* ☎ 020/488-7778. $$.

Brouwersgracht canal is lined with houseboats.

Amsterdam's **Jewish Quarter**

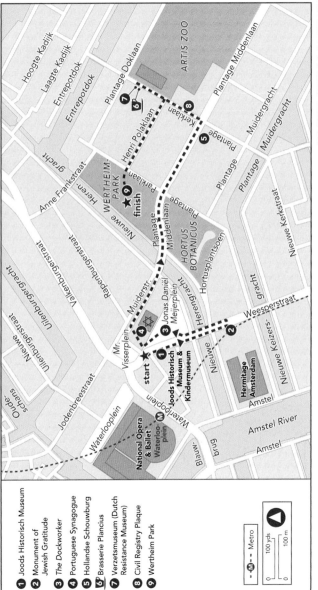

1 Joods Historisch Museum
2 Monument of Jewish Gratitude
3 The Dockworker
4 Portuguese Synagogue
5 Hollandse Schouwburg
6 Brasserie Plancius
7 Verzetsmuseum (Dutch Resistance Museum)
8 Civil Registry Plaque
9 Wertheim Park

100 yds
100 m

- M - Metro

Amsterdam's Jewish Quarter lies to the east of the old city center around the Plantage. Before World War II, this was a bustling area crammed with shops and businesses. The Waterlooplein market lay at the heart of the Jewish district and the synagogues formed the focus of the community. The atrocities of World War II saw that community decimated and mass deportations led to imprisonment and mass murder in Nazi concentration camps. Today the Jewish Cultural Quarter is full of memorials to those dark days. START: Tram 9 or 14 to Waterlooplein.

An exhibit from the Jewish Historical Museum.

❶ ★ Joods Historisch Museum (Jewish Historical Museum). This vast complex was central to Jewish life in Amsterdam between the 17th and mid-20th centuries as it originally consisted of four synagogues. Built by Ashkenazi Jewish refugees from Germany and Poland in the 17th and 18th centuries, it was sheer luck that they survived the Nazi occupation. The museum displays some of the artifacts looted from the Jewish community during the war; attempts have been made to enliven the displays with some interactive screens and personal commentary. The adjoining **Kindermuseum ★★** (Children's Museum) is cleverly set up as the home of a Jewish family, giving kids the chance to bake matzos, learn Yiddish, or celebrate the Sabbath. It's strictly a child-only zone. Museum tickets are also valid in the Portuguese Synagogue and Hollandse Schouwburg. ⏱ 1½ hr. Nieuwe Amstelstraat 1. ☎ 020/531-0310. www.jhm.nl. Admission 12€ adults,

6€ students and kids 13–17, 3€ kids 6–12. Daily 11am–5pm. Closed Apr 27, Rosh Hashanah, and Yom Kippur *(check online as dates change)*.

❷ ★ Monument of Jewish Gratitude. Just down Weesperstraat, once a busy shopping street at the heart of the Jewish Quarter, is the white limestone memorial given in thanks by the Jewish community to the people of Amsterdam for supporting them against the Nazis. It sits at the rear of the Hermitage Amsterdam (see p 17). *Weesperstraat.*

❸ ★★ The Dockworker. Back up Weesperstraat, walk across Mr.

Walking tours are available to see the Monument of Jewish Gratitude.

Nazis in The Netherlands

When the Germans arrived by invitation in Amsterdam on May 16, 1940, after intense bombing of Rotterdam, they were welcomed as the allies and saviors of The Netherlands. But slowly the Nazis clamped down on the city and its open-minded people; more brutal laws were enforced taking away individual freedom, and underground resistance to the Nazis mounted. The 10% of the population that was Jewish were persecuted, forced to wear yellow Stars of David, and stripped of their jobs. In 1942, the roundup of Jewish families began; thousands of people were taken to the Hollandse Schouwburg before being deported to labor camps, Bergen-Belsen in Germany, or Auschwitz in Poland. Of the 140,000 Sephardic and Ashkenazi Jews who lived in Amsterdam before World War II, less than 30,000 survived until Liberation on May 5, 1945. The most famous Dutch victim of the Holocaust was Anne Frank, whose tragic story is told at the Anne Frank Huis (see p 11) on Prinsengracht.

Visserplein toward the Portuguese Synagogue. Just to the left side of the complex is Jonas Daniël Meijerplein, where many Jews were herded while waiting to be deported to the concentration camps. The bronze figure surrounded by wreaths of flowers is by Mari Andriessen and was erected in 1952 in commemoration of the February 1941 strike by workers protesting against the deportations, which was violently suppressed by the Nazis. *Jonas Daniël Meijerplein.*

A statue to commemorate the dockworker strike of 1941.

❹ ★★ Portuguese Synagogue.
Across the street from the Jewish Museum stands Europe's largest synagogue (1675), constructed by Sephardic Jews from Spain and Portugal. The building was restored in the 1950s and today it looks essentially as it did 3 centuries ago. The women's gallery is supported by 12 stone columns representing the Twelve Tribes of Israel and the large, low-hanging brass chandeliers together hold 1,000 candles. In the courtyard are the *mikvah* ritual baths; the mourning room with coffin stand; and the synagogue's treasure chambers containing precious *menorahs*,

torahs, and ornate clerical robes.
🕐 *30 min. Mr. Visserplein 3.* ☎ *020/531-0380. www.portugesesynagoge.nl. Admission with ticket from Jewish Historical Museum 12€ adults, 6€ students and kids 13–17, 3€ kids 6–12. Apr–Oct Sun–Thurs 10am–5pm, Fri 10am–4pm; Nov–Mar Sun–Thurs 10am–4pm, Fri 10am–2pm. Closed Apr 27, Rosh Hashanah, and Yom Kippur (check online as dates change).*

❺ ★★ Hollandse Schouwburg.
From the synagogue, turn right past the **Hortus Botanicus** (see p 35), cross over the Nieuwe Herengracht

bridge and walk down Plantage Middenlaan to the Hollandse Schouwburg on your right. This imposing white building was originally a theater, but hundreds of Jewish families were forcibly detained here before deportation. It's now the official memorial to the Nazi Holocaust in Amsterdam, with a deeply moving documentary describing the persecution of the Jews. The small museum upstairs is mainly notable for its pictures of the hiding places used to conceal people from the Nazis. However, it is the monument out in the courtyard that grabs attention; a simple cast column scattered with flowers. ⏱ *45 min. Plantage Middenlaan 24.* ☎ *020/531-0310. www.hollandscheschouwburg.nl. Admission with ticket from Jewish Historical Museum 12€ adults, 6€ students and kids 13–17, 3€ kids 6–12. Daily 11am–5pm. Closed Apr 27, Rosh Hashanah, and Yom Kippur (check online as dates change).*

The interior of the Portuguese Synagogue.

🍵 ★★★ **Brasserie Plancius.** One of the most popular restaurants in the Plantage does a roaring trade in chicken saté, fries, burgers, and mega-salads. *Plantage Kerklaan 61.* ☎ *020/330-9469. www.brasserie plancius.nl. $$.*

❼ ★★★ **Verzetsmuseum (Dutch Resistance Museum).** One step beyond the brasserie, and with its entrance right opposite Artis Royal Zoo, is Amsterdam's Dutch Resistance Museum, where clever dioramas and interactive exhibits neatly unfold the absorbing story of the gradual rise of Dutch resistance to their Nazi occupiers. Printing presses, ID cards, and touching personal artifacts such as the Christmas tree made out of blackout curtains add to this impressive exhibition. About 20,000 Dutch were sent to labor camps in Germany; of those, 2,000 were executed and several thousand more did not survive. The Resistance Museum Junior is found in a new wing of the museum and focuses on the experience of children under Nazi occupation. ⏱ *90 min. Plantage Kerklaan 61.* ☎ *020/620-2535. Admission 8€ adults, 4.50€ kids 7–15. Tues–Fri 10am–5pm, Sat–Sun and public holidays 11am–5pm. Closed Jan 1, Apr 27, and Dec 25.*

❽ ★ **Civil Registry Plaque.** A plaque on the zoo wall opposite the Resistance Museum marks the Civil Registry, which held the names of around 70,000 Jews in the early 1940s. The registry was torched by 14 members of the Resistance on March 27, 1942. *Plantage Kerklaan.*

❾ ★ **Wertheim Park.** From the Dutch Resistance Museum, walk up Henri Polaklaan to a little scrap of grass overlooking Nieuwe Herengracht. In the center of Wertheim Park is a memorial (1993) by sculptor Jan Wolkers, dedicated to the victims of Auschwitz. Six large cracked-glass pieces laid flat on the ground reflect a shattered sky and cover a buried urn containing ashes of the dead from the concentration camp. The glass memorial reads, NOOIT MEER AUSCHWITZ ("Never again, Auschwitz"), with the words reflecting back from the glass. *Plantage Middenlaan.* ●

Shopping **Best Bets**

Best **Wine Store**
★ Wijnhandel De Ware Jacob, *Herenstraat 41 (p 76)*

Best **Antiques**
★★ Premsela & Hamburger, *Pieter Cornelisz Hooftstraat (p 70)*

Best **Delftware**
★★ Jorrit Heinen, *Prinsengracht 440 (p 72)*

Best **English-Language Bookstore**
★ American Book Center, *Spui 12 (p 70)*

Best **Place to Score Castro's Favorite Stogies**
★ P.G.C. Hajenius, *Rokin 92–96 (p 71)*

Best **Place to Shop for Diamonds**
★★★ Gassan Diamonds, *Nieuwe Uilenburgerstraat 173–175 (p 74)*

Best **Place to Pick Up Authentic Hunks of Gouda**
★★★ De Kaaskamer van Amsterdam, *Runstraat 7 (p 71)*

Best **Designer Shoes**
★★ United Nude, *Spuistraat 125a (p 76)*

Best **Street Market**
★★★ Albert Cuypmarkt, *Albert Cuypstraat (p 75)*

Best **Place to Provision for Romance**
★★ E. Kramer-Pontifex, *Reestraat 18–20 (p 71)*

Best **Place to Stop and Smell the Flowers**
★★ Bloemenmarkt (Flower Market), *along the south bank of Singel between Muntplein and Koningsplein (p 75)*

Best **Place to Shop for Picnic Provisions**
★ Boerenmarkt (Farmers Market), *Noordermarkt (p 76)*

Best **Place to Shop for Gifts for Friends Back Home**
★★★ 't Curiosa Winkeltje, *Prinsengracht 228 (p 74)*

Best **Department Store**
★★ de Bijenkorf, *Dam 1 (p 72)*

Best **Designer Boutique for Men, Women & Teens**
★★ Azzurro Due, *Pieter Cornelisz Hooftstraat 138 (p 72)*

Best **Unusual Kids' Toys**
★★★ Tinkerbell, *Spiegelgracht 10–12 (p 75)*

Best **Designer Goods at Discount Prices**
★★★ Megazino, *Rozengracht 207–213 (p 73)*

Best **Artisan Chocolates**
★ Puccini Bomboni, *Staalstraat 17 (p 71)*

Previous page: Magna Plaza's elegant interior.
This page: An antique silver spoon set and platter.

Museum District **Shopping**

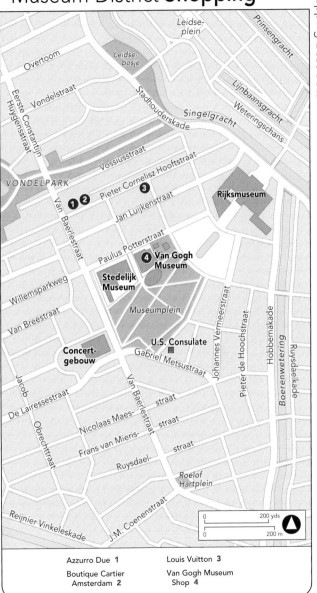

Azzurro Due **1**

Boutique Cartier
Amsterdam **2**

Louis Vuitton **3**

Van Gogh Museum
Shop **4**

Central Amsterdam **Shopping**

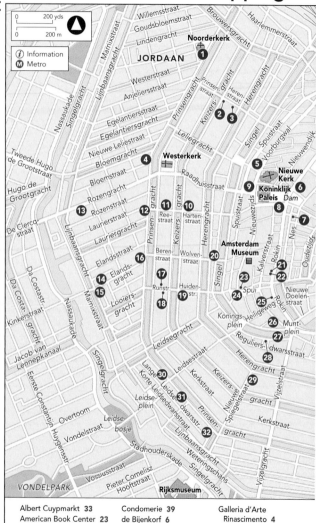

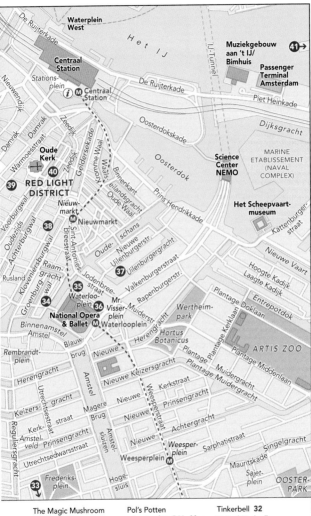

The Magic Mushroom
  Gallery **28**
Magna Plaza **9**
Mathieu Hart **25**
Megazino **13**
Noordermarkt
  op Zaterdag **1**
Peek & Cloppenburg **8**
P.G.C. Hajenius **21**

Pol's Potten
  Amsterdam B.V. **41**
Premsela &
  Hamburger **22**
Puccini Bomboni **34**
Redlight Fashion
  Amsterdam **40**
Smokiana **31**
't Curiosa Winkeltje **12**

Tinkerbell **32**
United Nude **5**
Van Ravenstein **19**
Waterlooplein
  Flea Market **36**
Webers Holland **38**
Wijnhandel De Ware
  Jacob **2**

The Best Shopping

Amsterdam Shopping A to Z

If you can't afford the real thing, shop for prints, reproductions, and more at the Van Gogh Museum Shop.

Art & Antiques

★★ Galerie Lieve Hemel

CANAL RING   In the Spiegelkwartier (see p 56), this gallery sells the best of contemporary Dutch art, bringing the still-life genre up to date, as well as lovely silver vases and tea services. *Nieuwe Spiegelstraat 3.* ☎ *020/623-0060. www.lievehemel.nl. Tram: 7 or 10 to Spiegelgracht. Map p 68.*

★★ Mathieu Hart OLD CENTER

Since 1878, this refined store has been selling color etchings of Dutch cities, rare old prints, 18th-century Delftware, and grandfather clocks. *Rokin 122.* ☎ *020/623-1658. www.hartantiques.com. Tram: 1, 2, 4, 5, 9, 14, 16, or 24 to Spui. Map p 69.*

Peruse thousands of books at the American Book Center.

★★ Premsela & Hamburger

OLD CENTER   Opened in 1823, this fine jewelry and antique silver seller boasts a great collection of Old Dutch silver by 17th-century craftsmen. *Rokin 98.* ☎ *020/624-9688. www.premsela.com. Tram: 1, 2, 4, 5, 9, 14, 16, or 24 to Spui. Map p 69.*

★★★ Van Gogh Museum Shop MUSEUM DISTRICT   This

starry store sells items such as imitations of Van Gogh classics, mugs painted with his famous sunflowers, and art books. *Paulus Potterstraat 7.* ☎ *020/570-5200. www.vangoghmuseum.nl. Tram: 2, 3, 5, or 12 to Van Baerlestraat; 16 or 24 to Museumplein. Map p 67.*

Books

★ American Book Center OLD

CENTER   From novels and Frommer's guides to the latest magazines, this large U.S.-style bookstore is extremely well stocked. *Spui 12.* ☎ *020/625-5537. www.abc.nl. Tram: 1, 2, 4, 5, 9, 14, 16, or 24 to Spui. Map p 68.*

★ Evenaar CANAL RING   Special-

izing in travel literature, this store has travel guides and world maps, books on armchair travel and anthropology, antique travel books, and more. *Singel 348.* ☎ *020/624-6289.*

You may have a hard time choosing from the hundreds of cheeses for sale at De Kaaskamer van Amsterdam.

www.evenaar.net. Tram: 1, 2, 4, 5, 9, 14, 16, or 24 to Spui. Map p 68.

Candles
★★ E. Kramer-Pontifex CANAL RING
All kinds of candles, from elaborately carved melting works of art to kitsch designs. Pick up scented candles and votives for a romantic evening in your hotel room. *Reestraat 20 (at Prinsengracht).* ☎ 020/626-5274. http://sites.google.com/site/pontifexkramer/home. Tram: 13, 14, or 17 to Westermarkt. Map p 68.

Cheese
★★★ De Kaaskamer van Amsterdam CANAL RING
Amsterdam's most famous cheese emporium is in the Nine Streets shopping district (see p 55). Choose from more than 300 cheeses (they vacuum-pack for travelers), including rows of Gouda wheels stamped with their farm of origin. *Runstraat 7 (at Keizersgracht).* ☎ 020/623-3483. www.kaaskamer.nl. Tram: 1, 2, 4, 5, 9, 14, 16, or 24 to Spui. Map p 68.

Chocolates
★ Puccini Bomboni OLD CENTER
A long, open table supports fresh handmade pralines in a plethora of shapes and styles—pure, milk, and white, as well as liqueur-filled and alcohol-free varieties. Two other branches are at Ouderkerksplein 17a and Singel 184. *Staalstraat 17.* ☎ 020/626-5474. www.puccini bomboni.com. Tram: 9 or 14 to Waterlooplein. Map p 69.

Cigars & Pipes
★ P.G.C. Hajenius OLD CENTER
In business since 1826, this store is the best place to shop for Cuban cigars—there's an entire room stocked with Havanas. You'll also find Dutch handmade clay pipes. *Rokin 92–96.* ☎ 020/623-7494. www.hajenius.com. Tram: 1, 2, 4, 5, 9, 14, 16, or 24 to Spui. Map p 69.

★★ Smokiana CANAL RING
In addition to pipe tobacco, this pipe store sells just about every kind of pipe imaginable, from the antique to the exotic to the kitsch to the downright weird. The store also hosts a bizarrely compelling pipe museum (see p 55). *Prinsengracht 488.* ☎ 020/421-1779. www.pijpenkabinet.nl. Tram: 1, 2, or 5 to Prinsengracht. Map p 69.

Delftware
★★ Galleria d'Arte Rinascimento CANAL RING
This emporium sells porcelain of every type,

Cigar lovers can pick up some fine Cubans in Amsterdam.

Hand-painted Delftware makes a great gift.

from quality-challenged blue-and-white pottery to genuine hand-painted Delftware from Koninklijke Porceleyne Fles (Royal Delft Porcelain Factory, see p 143), along with multicolored, and pricey, Makkum-ware from Koninklijke Tichelaar Makkum. *Prinsengracht 170 (at Bloemstraat).* ☎ *020/622-7509. www.delft-art-gallery.com. Tram: 13, 14, or 17 to Westermarkt. Map p 68.*

★★ **Jorrit Heinen** CANAL RING This family-owned chain makes and sells their own porcelain, and is also an official dealer of Delftware, Makkumware, fine crystal, and other quality gifts. *Prinsengracht 440 (at Leidsestraat).* ☎ *020/627-8299. www.delftsblauwwinkel.nl. Tram: 1, 2, or 5 to Prinsengracht. Map p 68.*

Department Stores
★★ **de Bijenkorf** OLD CENTER The city's best-known department store sports the largest variety of goods. From handbags to big-screen TVs, it's all here. *Dam 1.* ☎ *0800-0818. www.debijenkorf. nl. Tram: 1, 2, 4, 5, 9, 13, 14, 16, 17, or 24 to the Dam. Map p 68.*

★ **HEMA** OLD CENTER This smaller store is a great place to find

Amsterdam is a great place to shop for home furnishings.

basics like toothbrushes, kitchen accessories, and back-to-school stationery for kids. *Kalvertoren, Kalverstraat 212 (at Muntplein).* ☎ *020/311-4800. www.hema.nl. Tram: 4, 9, 14, 16, or 24 to Muntplein. Map p 68.*

★★ **Peek & Cloppenburg** OLD CENTER This shop does fashion for both sexes brilliantly at a range of price levels. Designer brands such as D&G and Armani mingle in with Fred Perry and Geox. *Dam 20.* ☎ *020/623-2837. www.peek-cloppenburg.nl. Tram: 1, 2, 4, 5, 9, 13, 14, 16, 17, or 24 to the Dam. Map p 69.*

Design & Home Furnishings
★★ **Pol's Potten Amsterdam B.V.** KNSM-EILAND This colorful interior-design store in the redeveloping Eastern Harbor area is a good place for furnishings, accessories, kitchenware, and household knickknacks by hip young designers. *KNSM-Laan 39.* ☎ *020/419-3541. www.polspotten.nl. Tram: 10 to Azartplein. Map p 69.*

Fashion
★★ **Azzurro Due** MUSEUM DISTRICT The ultimate address for finding a pair of designer jeans or that elusive Prada accessory for men and women. Very

chic, very trendy. *Pieter Cornelisz Hooftstraat 138.* ☎ *020/671-9708. www.azzurrofashiongroup.nl. Tram: 2, 3, 5, or 12 to Van Baerlestraat. Map p 67.*

★★ De Maagd & De Leeuw

CANAL RING This pretty boutique in the lovely Nine Streets shopping enclave sells jeans and stylish tops for off-duty wear, smart day dresses, and elegant gowns for the evening, all sourced from the latest Paris fashions. There's also a selection of stylish shoes and boots, belts in many colors, and leather bags at reasonable prices. *Hartenstraat 32.* ☎ *020/428-0047. www.demaagden-deleeuw.nl. Tram: 13, 14, or 17 to Westerkerk. Map p 68.*

★ Louis Vuitton MUSEUM

DISTRICT Of course, you'll find the usual upmarket suitcases and handbags here, but also a good selection of shoes, jewelry, belts, and ties. Another branch is at Dam 1. *Pieter Cornelisz Hooftstraat 65–67.* ☎ *020/575-5775. www.louisvuitton. com. Tram: 2, 3, 5, or 12 to Van Baerlestraat. Map p 67.*

★★★ Megazino JORDAAN

Large for Amsterdam, this designer outlet at Nine Streets sells discounted clothes for men and women from Armani, Gucci, and Prada to Calvin Klein and Dolce & Gabbana—all at 30% to 50% off the original price. *Rozengracht 207–213.* ☎ *020/ 330-1031. www.nlstreets.nl/NL/ winkel/megazino-store. Tram: 13, 14, or 17 to Westermarkt. Map p 69.*

★★ Redlight Fashion Amsterdam

With the ongoing cleanup of the Red Light District (see p 45), several of the prostitutes' windows in De Wallen have closed, and shops, exhibition spaces, galleries, and studios have appeared among the tawdry sex shops. Run by talented independent designers as part of Redlight Fashion

Shoppers can find all sorts of designer goods in Amsterdam, like these purses from Azzurro Due.

Amsterdam, stores to check out include Code on Oudezijds Achterburgwal for hot menswear designers at decent prices, and Jouw Stoute Schoenen on the same street for über-cool footwear. *www. redlightfashionamsterdam.com. Tram: 1, 2, 4, 5, 9, 13, 14, 16, 17, or 24 to the Dam. Map p 69.*

★★ Van Ravenstein CANAL RING

The latest creations by Dutch and Belgian designers and fashion houses, such as Ann Demeulemeester, Maison Martin Margiela, Dries Van Noten, and more, are the stock-in-trade of this small Nine Streets boutique. *Keizersgracht 359 (at Huidenstraat).* ☎ *020/639-0067. www.van-ravenstein.nl. Tram: 1, 2, or 5 to Keizersgracht. Map p 69.*

★ Webers Holland OLD CENTER

The venerable 17th-century Klein Trippenhuis (Little Trippenhuis), one of the narrowest houses in Amsterdam, is the counterintuitive setting for this avant-garde, sexy, humorous—and, to a degree, in-your-face—store for women. *Kloveniersburgwal 26.* ☎ *020/638-1777. www.webersholland.nl. Metro: Nieuwmarkt. Map p 69.*

Flowers
★★ Bloomings-Amsterdam

CANAL RING Orchids and other exotic plants, oriental lilies, special

The Best Shopping

tropical flowers, and all kinds of tasteful accessories give this Westerpark store a delicate look to go along with the scents. *Lucellestraat 20.* ☎ *06/2421-3723. www.bloomings-amsterdam.nl. Tram: 7, 10, or 17 to Elandsgracht. Map p 68.*

★★★ Gerda's Bloemen & Planten CANAL RING This elegant
florist at Nine Streets boasts a fantastic selection of exotic flowers and unusual plants artfully arranged and presented. *Runstraat 16.* ☎ *020/624-2912. www.theninestreets.com/gerda.html. Tram: 1, 2, 4, 5, 9, 14, 16, or 24 to Spui. Map p 68.*

Funky Stores
★ Condomerie OLD CENTER Handily situated on the edge of the Red Light District, this condom boutique stocks a vast range of these singular items, in all shapes, sizes, and flavors, from common brands to flashy designer fittings. *Warmoesstraat 141 (behind de Bijenkorf).* ☎ *020/627-4174. condomerie.com. Tram: 1, 2, 4, 5, 9, 13, 14, 16, 17, or 24 to the Dam. Map p 68.*

★★★ Episode WATERLOOPLEIN
Find jackets, dresses, scarves, belts, funky brooches, and boots at this unisex vintage store. Specialties include flamboyant evening gowns and leather jackets, all in good shape and reasonably priced. A second store is at Berenstraat 1.

Amsterdam's florists sell fresh bouquets and flower arrangements.

Waterlooplein 1. ☎ *020/320-3000. www.episode.eu. Tram: 9 or 14 to Waterlooplein. Map p 68.*

★★★ 't Curiosa Winkeltje
CANAL RING This funky but fun store sells old tin cars, glitzy gold tea services, plastic tulips in plastic pots, and children's toys from the 1950s. *Prinsengracht 228.* ☎ *020/625-1352. Tram: 13, 14, or 17 to Westermarkt. Map p 69.*

★★ The Magic Mushroom Gallery CANAL RING This smart
shop (see p 44) sells everything from "psychoactive mushrooms" to tonics such as Yohimbe Rush and Horn E that allegedly improve your sex life. *Spuistraat 249.* ☎ *020/427-5765. www.magicmushroom.com. Tram: 1, 2, 4, 5, 9, 14, 16, or 24 to Spui. Map p 69.*

Jewelry
★ Boutique Cartier Amsterdam MUSEUM DISTRICT You'll find intricately designed jewelry, watches, pens, and other accessories at this quintessential French store. *Pieter Cornelisz Hooftstraat 132–134.* ☎ *020/670-3434. www.cartier.com. Tram: 2, 3, 5, or 12 to Van Baerlestraat. Map p 67.*

★★★ Gassan Diamonds OLD
CENTER In addition to shopping for diamonds, you can take a tour in the stunning Amsterdam School–style building that shows you how the jewels are cut. Another store is at Rokin 1–5. *Nieuwe Uilenburgerstraat 173–175.* ☎ *020/622-5333. www.gassandiamonds.nl. Tram: 9 or 14 to Waterlooplein. Map p 68.*

★★ Gort CANAL RING This
beautiful little store specializes in unique and innovative jewelry. If you like modern and minimalist designs, then this place is for you. *Herenstraat 11.* ☎ *020/620-6240. www.juweliergort.nl. Tram: 13, 14, or 17 to Westermarkt. Map p 68.*

Kids
★★★ Tinkerbell CANAL RING
This unique store on the edge of
the Spiegelkwartier sells lovely and
cuddly teddy bears and old wooden
toys. It's a great place to find an
unusual gift for a child. *Spiegelgracht 10.* ☎ *020/625-8830. www.
tinkerbelltoys.nl. Tram: 7 or 10 to
Spiegelgracht. Map p 69.*

Malls
★★ Magna Plaza OLD CENTER
Housed in the city's former main
post office, built in 1899, this elegant
mall with four floors has just had a
multimillion-euro facelift. Stores
include Swarovski and the Spanish
fashion chain Mango. *Nieuwezijds
Voorburgwal 182.* ☎ *020/570-3570.
www.magnaplaza.nl. Tram: 1, 2, 5,
13, 14, or 17 to the Dam. Map p 69.*

Markets
★★★ Albert Cuypmarkt DE PIJP
Amsterdam's most-frequented all-
purpose street market stretches for
1km (½ mile). From fresh herring and
Gouda to silk scarves and hand-
knitted hats, you'll find it here Monday to Saturday 9am to 5pm. *Albert
Cuypstraat between Ferdinand Bolstraat & Van Woustraat. No phone.
www.albertcuypmarkt.nl. Tram: 4, 16,
or 24 to Albert Cuypstraat. Map p 68.*

★★ Antiekcentrum Amsterdam
JORDAAN   Formerly known as De
Looier, this large indoor art-and-
antiques market spreads throughout
several old warehouses. You'll find
everything from furniture and old
armoires to 19th-century tin toys, Delft
tiles, Dutch knickknacks, and antique
jewelry. Open Monday, Wednesday,
and Friday 11am to 6pm, Saturday
and Sunday 10am to 5pm. *Elandsgracht 109.* ☎ *020/624-9038. www.
antiekcentrumamsterdam.nl. Tram: 7,
10, or 17 to Elandsgracht. Map p 68.*

★ Artplein Spui OLD CENTER
Every Sunday (10am–6pm) from
March to December, local artists

*Gassan Diamonds offers an informative
tour in addition to dazzling jewelry.*

mount outdoor exhibits. You may
have to wade through some medi-
ocrity, but it's possible to find something special. *Spui.* ☎ *06/2499-2403.
www.artplein-spui.org. Tram: 1, 2, 4,
5, 9, 14, 16, or 24 to Spui. Map p 68.*

**★★ Bloemenmarkt (Flower
Market)** CANAL RING   Partly
floating on a row of permanently
moored barges, this is Amsterdam's most popular flower market
(see p 19). You'll find fresh-cut flowers, bright plants, rows and rows of
tulip bunches, and ready-to-travel
packets of tulip bulbs. Open Monday through Saturday 9am to
5:30pm, Sunday 11am to 5:30pm.
*Along the south bank of Singel
between Muntplein and Koningsplein. No phone. Tram: 9, 14, 16, or*

*A vendor sells poffertjes, a small fluffy
pancake, at the Albert Cuypmarkt.*

24 to Muntplein; 1, 2, or 5 to Koningsplein. Map p 68.

★ Boerenmarkt (Farmers Market) JORDAAN

Also known as the Bio (or organic) market, it caters to trendy Jordaan locals. It's a great place to find fresh vegetables, fruit, cheeses, and organic breads for a picnic. Open Saturday 9am to 4pm on Noordermarkt. It is surrounded by a flea market (see Noordermarkt op Zaterdag below). *Noordermarkt. No phone. www.boerenmarktamsterdam.nl. Tram: 3 or 10 to Marnixplein. Map p 68.*

★★ Noordermarkt op Zaterdag (Northern Market on Saturday) JORDAAN

The Noorderkerk (north church) was built in 1623, the final masterpiece of Hendrik de Keyser. The square surrounding this neo-Renaissance church is home to a sprawling flea market on Saturday. Stalls are a mixed bag of decent paintings, a few antiques, handmade jewelry, rugs, and old books at rock-bottom prices. Everything starts to close up around 2pm so get there at 9am to snap up some great vintage finds. The Bio market (see above) is adjacent. *Noordermarkt. No phone. www.noordermarkt-amsterdam.nl. Tram: 3 or 10 to Marnixplein. Map p 69.*

You can buy a wide variety of wine at Wijnhandel De Ware Jacob.

★ Waterlooplein Flea Market WATERLOOPLEIN

The big daddy of Amsterdam street markets has everything from bargain-basement souvenirs to antiques, old CDs, leather jackets, and wool hats. Open Monday through Saturday from 9am to 5:30pm. *Waterlooplein. No phone. www.waterloopleinmarkt.nl. Tram: 9 or 14 to Waterlooplein. Map p 69.*

Shoes

★ Betsy Palmer OLD CENTER

There are no classic shoes, but an incredible collection of trendy women's footwear, from pretty ballet flats by Unisa to chunky platforms from UGG Australia. *Rokin 9–15. ☎ 020/422-1040. www.betsypalmer. com. Tram: 1, 2, 4, 5, 9, 13, 14, 16, 17, or 24 to the Dam. Map p 68.*

★★ United Nude CANAL RING

Wackily designed boutique selling massively trendy women's shoes. Styles have recently included some gravity-defying boots by architect Zaha Hadid. *Spuistraat 125a. ☎ 020/626-0010. www.unitednude. com. Tram: 1, 2, 4, 5, 9, 14, 16, or 24 to Spui. Map p 69.*

Soap

★★ kids La Savonnerie CANAL RING

Artisanal soaps of all shapes and sizes are sold here. The soap chess set makes a great gift. You can buy personalized soap and even make your own. Kids should enjoy the animal-shaped soaps. *Prinsengracht 294. ☎ 020/428-1139. www.savonnerie.nl. Tram: 7, 10, or 17 to Elandsgracht. Map p 68.*

Wine

★ Wijnhandel De Ware Jacob CANAL RING

Since 1970, this small but charming wine store has carried the finest wines from boutique wineries around the world. *Herenstraat 41. ☎ 020/623-9877. www.warejacob.com. Tram: 13, 14, or 17 to Westermarkt. Map p 69.* ●

Strolling in **Vondelpark**

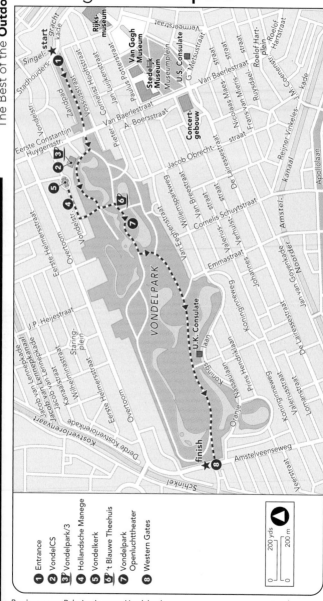

1 Entrance
2 VondelCS
3 Vondelpark/3
4 Hollandsche Manege
5 Vondelkerk
6 't Blauwe Theehuis
7 Vondelpark Openluchttheater
8 Western Gates

Previous page: Relaxing in green Vondelpark.

Central Amsterdam is a densely packed city, but several vast parks provide tranquil refuges from the crowds of tourists if not the marauding cyclists. Of these, Oosterpark is the oldest, the Westerpark is a hive of music and concerts, and Sarphatipark is Amsterdam's best-kept neighborhood secret, but the Vondelpark is the biggest and most loved. A step away from Museumplein, it encompasses 47 hectares (116 acres) of lawn set in an English-style park where manicured rose gardens and ponds are set amid trails for joggers, bikers, and in-line skaters. START: **Tram 1, 2, 5, 7, or 10 to Leidseplein.**

Vondelpark entrance.

❶ ★★ Main Entrance. Enter the park through the main gates at 1e Constantijn Huygensstraat, less than a 10-minute walk from Leidseplein. The sculpture *Maid of Amsterdam*, a symbol of the city, sits over these gates. The park opened to the public in 1865. Jan David Zocher and Louis David Zocher (a father-and-son operation) landscaped what was then a much smaller space, using rose gardens, ponds, and pathways to create an English-style garden. Over the years, as the park grew to its present size, some 130 different species of trees were planted. The park is home to squirrels, rabbits, wading birds, and a colony of bright-green parakeets. Wherever you walk in the park, keep to your right to avoid zooming bikes.

❷ VondelCS. From the gates, head south, keeping to the path on

VondelCS.

Vondelkerk.

3 Vondelpark/3. Vertigo's funky replacement in Vondelpark's spruced-up pavilion serves up a menu of finger foods, *broodjes* (sandwiches), and salads during the day, plus a la carte choices by night. The suntrap terraces are just the spot for alfresco summer dining. *Overtoom 34.* ☎ *020/639-2589. www.unlimitedlabel.com/en/vondelpark3. $$.*

your right. After about 500m (550 yards), you'll see this grand pavilion to your right. Constructed in a flamboyant Italian neo-Renaissance style, it opened in 1881 as a cafe and restaurant and then became an international cultural center in 1947. From 1972 until 2011, the pavilion housed the country's main film museum, **EYE Film Institute** (see p 29), which has a shiny new home on the north shore of the IJ. The pavilion is now run by Dutch broadcaster AVRO as a multimedia cultural center. The famous Vertigo cafe has gone, replaced by Vondelpark/3 in March 2014. *Vondelpark 3.*

4 Hollandsche Manege (Dutch Riding School). When you exit the cafe, stay on the path to the right and you'll see the glorious neoclassical facade of the Dutch Riding School, which was built in 1882 by A.L. van Gendt. Restored in the 1980s, it still operates as a stable and arena. The building was modeled after the Spanish Riding School in Vienna. A tour includes the vaulted *manège* with its orchestra pits, gilded mirrors, and molded horses' heads; the stables; and a short documentary. You can take lessons here; call ahead to book. *Vondelstraat 140 (on Overtoom).* ☎ *020/618-0942. www.dehollandschemanege.nl. Admission 8€ adults, 4€ kids 3–12. Daily 10am–5pm. Tram: 3 or 12 to Overtoom.*

Revitalizing Vondelpark

The 10 million-plus visitors to Vondelpark every year are seriously impacting the earth. The park was built on peat, and now the ground is 0.6m (2 ft.) lower than the surrounding buildings. Indeed, the VondelCS (see above) is at the city's lowest point, well below the water table. In the past, when it rained, some areas of the park were prone to collect water, resulting in large, unwanted ponds. A renovation project that ended in 2010 reconnected some of the older ponds and created a new drainage system. The landscapers also planted new varieties of water-absorbing trees and bushes.

Friday Night Skate

If you're game for a little rollerblading, try joining the many skaters (one time a record 3,000) who strap on their 'blades for Amsterdam's regular—and free—**Friday Night Skate** (www.friday nightskate.com). This event, which started in 1997, begins at 8:30pm, weather permitting, from outside the VondelCS in Vondelpark, and takes one of a series of possible routes through the city (around 20km, or 12½ miles), returning to the starting point. Wear a helmet and knee protection; you can rent blades from **De Vondeltuin** (☎ 06/2756-5576; www.devondeltuin.nl) on the southwest side of the park near the western gates leading on to Amstelveenseweg.

If you're up for it, join the hundreds of skaters who skate around the city for Friday Night Skate.

⑤ Vondelkerk. Close to the Riding School is a large Catholic church designed by Pierre Cuypers, architect of **Centraal Station** (see p 29) and the **Rijksmuseum** (see p 7). It was completed in 1880 but a fire in 1904 destroyed its original tower; a new one was added by the architect's son. In 1985, the church was converted into offices, but it can be rented for cultural events and weddings. *Vondelstraat 120-D. www.vondelkerk.nl.*

⑥ 't Blauwe Theehuis. "The Blue Teahouse" is a functionalist-style spaceship of a cafe. Its two levels include a park-level open-air terrace and an upstairs balcony terrace. It's a fine place for indulging in a coffee and croissant. At night, there's dancing and live music. *Vondelpark 5. ☎ 020/662-0254. www. blauwetheehuis.nl. $.*

⑦ ★ kids Vondelpark Openluchttheater (Vondelpark Open-Air Theater). Another few minutes' stroll brings you to the dome-shaped open-air stage, where summer music festivals, concerts, theater, and children's shows are staged free of charge. Performances take place Friday to Sunday from late May through the third week of August. Kids' drama courses are also run at the theater; check the website for program details. *Vondelpark 5a. ☎ 020/428-3360. www.openluchttheater.nl. Free admission.*

⑧ Western Gates. By the time you reach the western gates on Amstelveenseweg, you'll have walked a little over 2km (1¼ miles). You can exit here and jump on tram 1 from Overtoom or tram 2 from Koninginneweg to go back into the city, or you can head back east, staying to your right to take the path back to the entrance gates close to Leidseplein. The entire loop measures about 4km (2½ miles).

Touring Amsterdam by **Canal Bike**

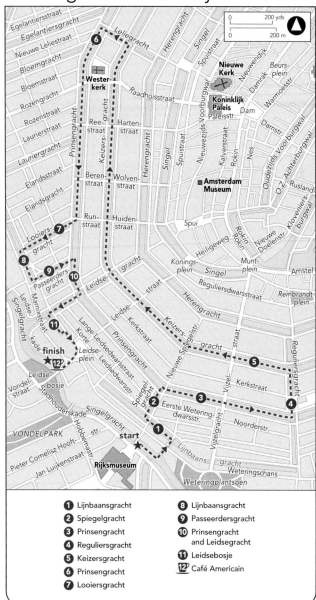

1 Lijnbaansgracht
2 Spiegelgracht
3 Prinsengracht
4 Reguliersgracht
5 Keizersgracht
6 Prinsengracht
7 Looiersgracht

8 Lijnbaansgracht
9 Passeerdersgracht
10 Prinsengracht and Leidsegracht
11 Leidsebosje
12 Café Americain

Canal biking down the city's myriad waterways is an outdoor activity peculiar to Amsterdam. These pedal boats (or pedalos) let you glide quietly down the canals for a close-up look at houseboats and bridges. You'll also get a different vantage point from which to admire the many 17th- and 18th-century houses that line the canals. Early on a summer's evening or late on a winter's afternoon is the best time for a trip, when the slanting sun hits the buildings and bridges, affording rich opportunities for photos.

START: **Tram 7 or 10 to Spiegelgracht for the Rijksmuseum mooring on the Singelgracht canal.**

❶ **Lijnbaansgracht.** From the Rijksmuseum mooring on Singelgracht, take a left into Lijnbaansgracht, with its very low bridge and rows of neck-gabled houses. This long canal goes all the way to Haarlemmerpoort, and is where 17th-century rope-makers (Lijnbaansgracht translates as "ropewalk") used to stretch and twist the ropes they made for the Dutch shipbuilding industry.

❷ ★ **Spiegelgracht.** Turn right onto this short canal lined with antiques shops. There are 100 or so specialized antiques dealers behind the gabled facades in the **Spiegelkwartier** neighborhood (see p 56),

Lijnbaansgracht canal.

You can get a close-up view of houseboats and canal houses from the seat of a canal bike.

selling everything from barometers and clocks to brass and copper ornaments. If you choose to stop and have a look, leave one person in your party with the canal bike—don't leave it unattended.

❸ ★★★ **Prinsengracht.** Turn right onto one of Amsterdam's Golden Age canals. Many of the houses here were built between 1635 and 1700. The houses along this stretch of the canal all belonged to rich families and have ornate facades and steps up to their doors—an indication of wealth.

❹ ★ **Reguliersgracht.** Turn left onto Reguliersgracht. Look forward to spot seven identical arched bridges, perfectly aligned, spanning this canal. These date back to

Reguliersgracht canal has seven identical arched bridges that are perfectly aligned.

the 17th century. It's a famous spot for photographs, and the waterway can get pretty crowded.

5 ★★★ **Keizersgracht.** Turn left onto Keizersgracht, the city's widest canal at 28m (92 ft.). Some of the houses lining the canal were built as coach houses for the mansions of the prosperous "Golden Bend" stretch of nearby Herengracht. You'll be pedaling for quite some time (30–45 min.) on Keizersgracht as you head northwards along the edge of the old city center and into the Jordaan. To begin looping back, turn left on tiny Leliegracht, and then left again on Prinsengracht.

6 ★★★ **Prinsengracht.** You are back on Prinsengracht, now in

You can spot the tall spire of the Westerkerk from Prinsengracht Canal.

the heart of the elegant and charming Jordaan neighborhood. The **Anne Frank Huis** (see p 11) is on the left, just before the tall spire of the **Westerkerk** (see p 54). You'll see many houseboats lining the banks of Prinsengracht; most of them have been here since just after World War II, when the housing shortage forced some people to find alternative dwellings. There are currently some 2,500 houseboats in Amsterdam, and they cost as much as houses on land to buy.

7 **Looiersgracht.** Turn right at the "Tanners' Canal"; not surprisingly, this is where leather was tanned.

8 **Lijnbaansgracht.** Turn left and you're back on to Lijnbaansgracht.

9 ★★★ **Passeerdersgracht.** Turn left here and notice the low railing on the bridge that stops cars from falling into the water. Before that was built, cars frequently fell into the canal, and in the 18th century, horses and carriages also tumbled into the water. Railings were not installed on any of Amsterdam's 100km (62 miles) of canals until the 1960s.

10 **Prinsengracht and Leidsegracht.** Turn right and you're on Prinsengracht again. Turn right onto Leidsegracht. Notice the four houses at nos. 72–78, which display four different kinds of gables: No.

Canal Bike Rentals & Rules

Canal bikes can seat up to four people (a child can be carried as a fifth passenger in some circumstances) and they are stable and comfortable. The charge per head is 8€ for 1 hour, 11€ for 1½ hours, and 14€ for 2 hours. The above itinerary will take about 2 hours. You'll need a credit card, a 20€ refundable deposit (which can go on the card), and an ID to rent your canal bike; a free map is given with every trip. Rental hours are 10am to between 6 and 9:30pm (depending on the weather) June to September; and 10am to 5:30pm the rest of the year (in winter, only when the weather is tolerable). Rent from **Canal Bike,** at the Rijksmuseum mooring on Singelgracht (☎ **020/217-0500;** www.canal.nl). In addition to this mooring, there are docks in front of the Anne Frank Huis on Prinsengracht, and at Leidseplein facing the American Hotel. If you get tired, drop off your canal bike at one of these moorings and get your deposit back.

Always stay to the right when navigating the canals—this is especially important when going under bridges in narrow canals. All other traffic has right of way. The port area and the Amstel River are off-limits to canal bikes. If you need a break, stop at one of the mooring docks. **Never** leave your canal bike unattended—it will be towed away.

72 has a neck gable, 74 a cornice gable, 76 a spout gable, and 78 a step gable (see p 30).

⓫ **Leidsebosje.** Turn left and you've reached the end! Return your canal bike here and head for a restorative drink at the Art Nouveau **American Hotel** (see below) opposite the mooring.

⓬ ★★ **Café Americain.** Overlooking Leidseplein, this cafe is a national monument to Dutch Art Nouveau. Don't forget to look up to admire the frosted-glass Tiffany chandeliers. There are plenty of salads, soups, and sandwiches to choose from. *Hampshire Amsterdam American Hotel, Leidsekade 97.* ☎ *020/556-3000. www.hampshire-hotels.com. $$.*

You'll spot many tour boats from the seat of your canal bike.

Biking Along the **Amstel River**

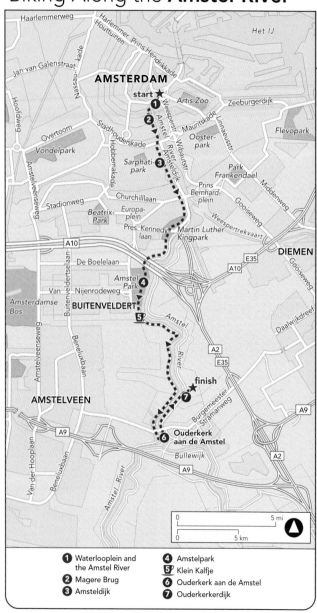

1 Waterlooplein and the Amstel River
2 Magere Brug
3 Amsteldijk
4 Amstelpark
5 Klein Kalfje
6 Ouderkerk aan de Amstel
7 Ouderkerkerdijk

Amsterdammers go everywhere on their bikes and don't make any concessions for inexperienced visitors on a rented *fiets* (bicycle in Dutch) who attempt to navigate the inner city's complicated streets, alleyways, and one-way systems while dodging the trams. This bike route takes you away from the city center and to the tranquil countryside. START: **Tram 9 or 14 to Waterlooplein.**

Traveling the city by bike is a way of life for many Amsterdammers.

❶ Waterlooplein and the Amstel River. Once you've rented your bikes (see the box "Renting Your Bikes," below), head south out of Waterlooplein; the **National Opera & Ballet** (see p 117) will be on your right. Making sure the Amstel is on your left, follow Amsteldijk; on your return, you'll be on the far bank, with the river again on your left. Look for **Hermitage Amsterdam** (see p 17), houseboats moored along both banks, and a lot of maritime bustle on the river.

❷ ★ Magere Brug (Skinny Bridge). The Skinny Bridge over the Amstel is an 18th-century replacement of the original 17th-century bridge. It's a double drawbridge that opens every 10 minutes or so to let river traffic through and is floodlit with hundreds of lights at night. The **Carré** (see p 119), one of the city's largest cultural venues, is visible from the bridge.

❸ Amsteldijk. As you pedal south, you'll need to negotiate busy Stadhouderskade. Continue on Amsteldijk south to the Berlagebrug (Berlage Bridge), where the traffic thickens again. Stay on Amsteldijk—most of the traffic swings away to the right on President Kennedylaan. The road becomes noticeably quieter, and you can relax and admire the many

Biking across the Skinny Bridge.

Enjoy peaceful views of the canals, rivers, and parks as you pedal through the city.

houseboats lined up along the river.

4 Amstelpark. Go under the highway bridge (A10 ring road) and continue along the riverbank until you reach this tranquil park. Continue south until you see the Rieker windmill, built in 1636, and a bronze statue of Rembrandt, who used to sketch the landscapes here. Look for storks' nests, pheasants, and squirrels. It's a perfect spot for a rest and a photo or two, so stretch your legs and have a snack.

5 Klein Kalfje. This traditional Dutch cafe-restaurant has a great sheltered terrace along the water (separated from the restaurant by the riverside road). Try the Dutch pea soup or a filling salad and fuel up for your ride back with a strong Dutch coffee. *Amsteldijk-Noord 355.* ☎ *020/644-5338. www.restaurant kleinkalfje.nl. $$.*

6 ★ Ouderkerk aan de Amstel. Ride south past villas and cottages to this charming little village. If you have time, lock up your bikes and meander the village streets before heading back; check out the De Zwaan windmill, the brightly painted gabled cottages, and the Beth Haim Jewish cemetery, the oldest in The Netherlands.

7 Ouderkerkerdijk. Head back north on the opposite bank of the Amstel. This is quieter and narrower than the Amsteldijk, with much less traffic. Turn left across Spaklerweg and left again onto Omval. When you reach the Berlagebrug and the road name changes to Weesperzijde, you'll know you're getting close to your starting point. The streets are busier here, but stay on the right bank and enjoy the different city vistas until you reach Waterlooplein. ●

Renting Your Bikes

The rental outlet closest to your starting point is MacBike at Waterlooplein 199 (☎ **020/428-7005;** www.macbike.nl). To get there, take tram 9 or 14 or the metro to Waterlooplein. You'll need ID and a 50€ refundable deposit per bike (cash or credit card). Rates (with insurance) are 9€ for 3 hours and 13€ for 1 day for a pedal-brake bike; 13€ and 18€ respectively, for a bike with a handbrake. MacBike is open daily 9am to 5:45pm. A range of bikes is available, including tandems, six-speed touring bikes, and kids bikes. There are four other MacBike outlets: on Stationsplein outside Centraal Station, Oosterdokskade 149, Weteringschans 2 at Leidseplein, and Marnixstraat 220.

Dining Best Bets

Best Wine List
★★ Christophe $$$$–$$$$$
Leliegracht 46 (p 95)

Best When Money Is No Object
★★★ La Rive $$$$$ *Professor Tulpplein 1 (p 97)*

Best for Laid-back Service
★★ Lof $$$$ *Haarlemmerstraat 62 (p 97)*

Best Place for Dining with Your Shoes Off
★ Supperclub $$–$$$ *Jonge Roelensteeg 21 (p 99)*

Best Indonesian Rijstaffel
★★ Tempo Doeloe $$–$$$ *Utrechtsestraat 75 (p 99)*

Best Innovative Five-Course Menu
★★ Bordewijk $$$–$$$$ *Noordermarkt 7 (p 94)*

Best Drop-Dead Gorgeous Decor
★★ Vinkeles $$$$$ *Keizersgracht 384 (p 100)*

Best Upmarket Moroccan Cuisine
★ Mamouche $$ *Quellijnstraat 104 (p 97)*

Best for Trendy Parents with No Babysitter
★★ Wilhelmina-Dok $$ *Nordwal 1 (p 100)*

Best for Cooking your Own Supper
★★ Miss Korea Barbecue $$
Albert Cuypstraat 66–70 (p 97)

Best Vegetarian
★★ Golden Temple $$
Utrechtsestraat 126 (p 96)

Best for Sinful Suppers
★★ Envy $$$$ *Prinsengracht 381 (p 96)*

Best for Fashionistas
★ Caffepc $$ *Pieter Cornelisz Hooftstraat 87 (p 95)*

Best for Dining Alfresco
★★ De Kas $$$$ *Kamerlingh Onneslaan 3 (p 95)*

Best for Kids
★ Pancake Bakery $–$$
Prinsengracht 191 (p 98)

Best for Late-Night Partying
★ Tapas & Crazy Cocktail Bar $$
Halvemaansteeg 8 (p 99)

Best Elegant Indonesian
★ Sama Sebo $$–$$$ *Pieter Cornelisz Hooftstraat 27 (p 98)*

Best for Pre-Concertgebouw Dining
★ Brasserie Keyzer $$$ *Van Baerlestraat 96 (p 94)*

Previous page: Dining canalside at Leidseplein.
This page: Dine like an Amsterdammer on raw herring and onions.

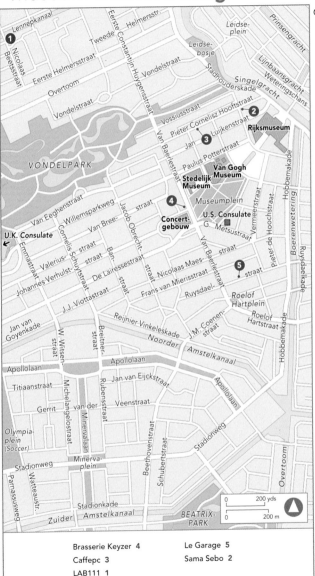

Museum District **Dining**

Brasserie Keyzer **4**
Caffepc **3**
LAB111 **1**

Le Garage **5**
Sama Sebo **2**

The Best Dining

Central Amsterdam Dining

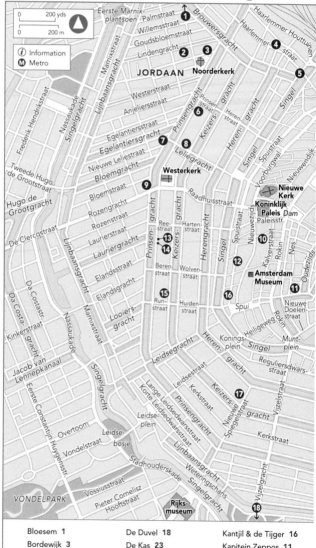

Bloesem 1	De Duvel 18	Kantjil & de Tijger 16
Bordewijk 3	De Kas 23	Kapitein Zeppos 11
Café-Restaurant Van Puffelen 13	De Prins 7	La Rive 22
	Envy 14	Lof 4
Christophe 8	Golden Temple 21	Mamouche 18

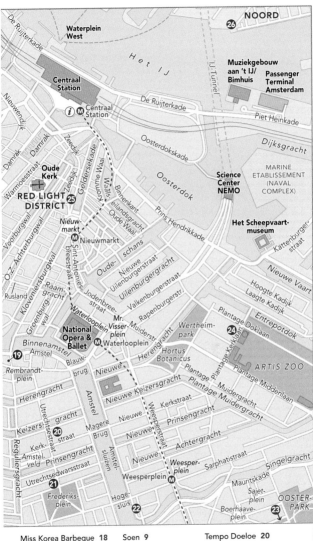

Miss Korea Barbeque 18	Soen 9	Tempo Doeloe 20
Nam Kee 25	Stubbe's Haring 5	Toscanini 2
Pancake Bakery 6	Supperclub 10	Vinkeles 15
Pasta e Basta 17	Tapas & Crazy	Visrestaurant Lucius 12
Plancius 24	Cocktail Bar 19	Wilhelmina-Dok 26

Amsterdam Restaurants A to Z

★ **Bloesem** OLD CENTER *FUSION* At hip Bloesem, the chef decides the menu each day, serving up an unusual brand of cuisine. The menu is set by the chef according to season: European fusion, with offerings such as watermelon gazpacho, duck confit with sauerkraut, or a Belgian endive salad with Valencia oranges. *Binnen Dommersstraat 13–15 (at Vinkenstraat).* ☎ 06/1445-6644. www.restaurant-bloesem.info. Fixed-price menus 33€–45€. Dinner Tues–Sun. Tram: 3 to Haarlemmerplein. Map p 92.

★★ **Bordewijk** JORDAAN *MODERN FRENCH* Trendy, affluent locals and laid-back gourmands come to this surprisingly casual restaurant for the creative French cuisine with Mediterranean accents, plus the superb wine lists. The chef takes time to explain the menu and take orders himself. In summer, you can dine alfresco on the canal. Reservations recommended. *Noordermarkt 7 (at Prinsengracht).* ☎ 020/624-3899. bordewijk.nl. Entrees 20€–30€; fixed-price menus 39€–54€.

Dinner Tues–Sat. Tram: 1, 2, 5, 13, or 17 to Martelaarsgracht. Map p 92.

★ **Brasserie Keyzer** MUSEUM DISTRICT *DUTCH/INTERNATIONAL* This classy, century-old brasserie with dark, dusky decor and starched pink linens serves fresh fish, hare, and venison in delicate style. The lunch menu is simpler: croquettes, salads, and scrambled eggs. *Van Baerlestraat 96.* ☎ 020/675-1866. www.brasseriekeyzer.nl. Entrees 18€–57€; fixed-price dinner 29€–37€. Breakfast, lunch, and dinner daily. Tram: 3, 5, 12, 16, or 24 to Museumplein. Map p 91.

★★ **Café-Restaurant Van Puffelen** CANAL RING *EUROPEAN* This brown cafe has grown to be a popular restaurant that rambles through two canal houses. Lunch is mainly Dutch staples; dinner sees Dutch and European dishes served, often with Asian twists, such as veal and oyster mushrooms served with noodles and peanut sauce. *Prinsengracht 375–377.* ☎ 020/624-6270. www.restaurantvanpuffelen.com. Entrees 18€–20€. Lunch Fri–Sun;

Be sure to sample a variety of Dutch cheeses while you're in Amsterdam.

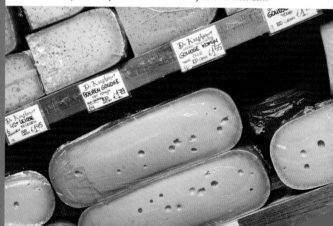

dinner daily. Tram: 13, 14, or 17 to Westermarkt. Map p 92.

★ **Caffepc** MUSEUM QUARTER *INTERNATIONAL* Smack in the middle of Amsterdam's most expensive shopping street, this is a decent breakfast spot before a visit to the **Rijksmuseum** (see p 7). At the end of the day, you can join models and fashion gurus to sip a martini while indulging in tapas and fresh salads. *Pieter Cornelisz Hooftstraat 87.* ☎ *020/639-2589. www. pchooftstraat.nl/caffepc. Entrees 14€–20€. Breakfast, lunch, and dinner daily; closed Sun–Wed 7pm, Thurs 10pm, Fri–Sat 8pm. Tram: 2 or 5 to Hobbemastraat. Map p 91.*

★★ **Christophe** CANAL RING *FRENCH/MEDITERRANEAN* Ultra-refined French cooking combined with unusual ingredients best describes the cuisine at French chef Jean-Joël Bonsens's elegant restaurant. The menu shows off North African and Italian elements complemented by an excellent wine list from knowledgeable sommelier Ellen Mansfield. Reservations required. *Leliegracht 46.* ☎ *020/ 625-0807. www.restaurantchristophe. nl. Entrees 29€–46€; fixed-price menus 36€–66€. Dinner Tues–Sat. Tram: 13, 14, or 17 to Westermarkt. Map p 92.*

★ **De Duvel** DE PIJP *INTERNATIONAL* Packed with hip and trendy locals, De Duvel (the Devil) serves excellent food in a cozy red dining room. Carpaccio with truffle oil and spicy prawns are two of the more popular dishes. You'll also find a daily selection of pasta, seafood, and Asian offerings. *Eerste Van der Helststraat 59–61.* ☎ *020/ 675-7517. www.deduvel.nl. Entrees 15€–20€. Lunch and dinner daily. Tram: 3 to 2e Van der Helststraat or 12 to Ferdinand Bolstraat. Map p 92.*

Stop for a cup of coffee or a beer at De Prins.

★★★ **De Kas** AMSTERDAM SOUTH *INTERNATIONAL* In summer, the huge outdoor patio seats more than 100 guests adjacent to fragrant herb gardens. The interior is light and spacious (it was formerly a greenhouse), beneath a vaulted glass ceiling. You get just a couple of variations on a three-course fixed menu that changes daily, and chef Jarno van den Broek makes extensive use of organic products and ingredients. Reservations recommended. *Kamerlingh Onneslaan 3, Park Frankendael.* ☎ *020/462-4562. www.restaurant dekas.nl. Fixed-price lunch 39€; fixed-price dinner 50€ (chef's table 130€). Lunch Mon–Fri; dinner Mon–Sat. Tram: 9 to Hogeweg. Map p 92.*

★★ **De Prins** CANAL RING *EUROPEAN* Relax with the locals at a popular traditional Dutch *eet-café* (cafe with food) just across the canal from the Anne Frank Huis. Choose from steaks, fondues, and burgers and take your pick from a great selection of Dutch and Belgian beers. There's sometimes live music at Sunday brunch. *Prinsengracht 124 (at Egelantiersgracht).*

☎ 020/624-9382. www.deprins.nl. Entrees 12€–18€. Lunch and dinner daily. Tram: 13, 14, or 17 to Westermarkt. Map p 92.

★★ **Envy** CANAL RING *MODERN ITALIAN* The emphasis at this bastion of cool is on grazing on small plates of food, tapas-style. Small but perfectly formed tuna, crab, risotto, sausage, and entrecôte dishes are all created in the open kitchen and most of the ingredients are organic. Guest chefs often make their appearance, and it's on its way to getting a coveted Michelin star. *Prinsengracht 381.* ☎ *020/344-6407. www.envy.nl. Entrees 9.50€–13€; tasting menu 35€. Lunch Fri–Sun; dinner daily. Tram: 13, 14, or 17 to Westerkerk. Map p 92.*

★★ **Golden Temple** CANAL RING *VEGETARIAN* This is one of the best vegetarian, vegan, and raw food options in town. Although the minimalist atmosphere is a tad too hallowed, the menu livens things up, with its unlikely roster of Indian and Middle Eastern plates, mung bean salads, and Italian pizza. Mixed *thalis* and *mezze* are the way to go. *Utrechtsestraat 126.* ☎ *020/626-8560. www.restaurantgolden temple.com. Entrees 14€–21€. Dinner daily. Tram: 4 to Prinsengracht. Map p 92.*

★★ **Kantjil & de Tijger** OLD CENTER *INDONESIAN* Unlike Holland's many Indonesian restaurants that wear their ethnic origins on their sleeves, with staffers decked out in traditional costume, the Antelope and the Tiger is chic and modern. A bestseller in this popular eatery is the 20-item rijsttafel (mixed rice dishes) for two; there's a takeaway service, too. Reservations recommended for Friday and Saturday evening. *Spuistraat 291–293.* ☎ *020/620-0994. www. kantjil.nl. Rijsttafels 25€–32€. Lunch and dinner daily. Tram: 1, 2, 4, 5, 9, 14, 16, or 24 to Spui. Map p 92.*

★★ **Kapitein Zeppos** OLD CENTER *FISH* A casual cafe tucked away down a little alley of Spui, Zeppos offers cheeses, salads, and great pots of mussels by day and feasts of Portuguese *mariscos* (seafood platter) or Coquille St-Jacques by night. There's live music most nights and kitsch sing-alongs the first Sunday brunch of the month in winter. *Gebed Zonder End 5, Spui.* ☎ *020/624-2057. www.zeppos.nl.*

Some of the 20 or so dishes you might find at an Indonesian rijsttafel.

Entrees 17€–24€. Lunch and dinner daily. Tram: 1, 2, 4, 5, 9, 14, 16, or 24 to Spui. Map p 92.

★ **LAB111** VONDELPARK DUTCH/ CONTINENTAL This self-described "media cafe" occupies the unlikely setting of a former pathology laboratory that now houses New Art Space Amsterdam, a contemporary arts center and art-house cinema. The restaurant's cool black-and-metal vibe is perked up by electric green tables, and the menu offers Mediterranean cuisine such as carpaccio or ravioli stuffed with goat's cheese. *Arie Biemondstraat 111.* ☎ 020/616-9994. www.lab111.nl. Entrees 17€–19€. Dinner daily. Tram: 1 to Jan Pieter Heijestraat, or 3 or 12 to Overtoom. Map p 91.

★★★ **La Rive** OOST FRENCH/ MEDITERRANEAN Service at the city's top-rated restaurant, helmed by Michelin-starred master chef Rogér Rassin, is tranquil and unobtrusive. In fact, you'll dine like royalty on dishes such as veal cheek with lentils, orange and chicory, or perfectly cooked Wagyu beef. Reservations required. *Amstel InterContinental Hotel, Professor Tulpplein 1 (off Weesperstraat).* ☎ 020/520-3264. www.restaurantlarive.nl. Fixed-price menu 95€–115€. Lunch and dinner daily. Tram: 7 or 10 to Sarphatistraat. Map p 92.

★ **Le Garage** MUSEUM DISTRICT POSH BRASSERIE Once the hottest restaurant in town, Le Garage has been under scrutiny recently for slipping standards of service; the jury is still out on this but the food is certainly holding up. Try tuna pizza or piles of oysters in a glitzy setting with bright lights and big mirrors that's reminiscent of Las Vegas. Reservations recommended. *Ruysdaelstraat 54–56 (at Van Baerlestraat).* ☎ 020/679-7176.

www.restaurantlegarage.nl. Entrees 23€–38€; fixed-price lunch 27€; fixed-price dinner 36€. Lunch Mon–Fri; dinner daily. Tram: 3, 5, 12, or 24 to Roelof Hartplein. Map p 91.

★★ **Lof** OLD CENTER INTERNATIONAL For all its unobtrusive persona, minimalist decor, and lack of urgency, Lof (the name is Dutch for "praise") is highly commendable. The roster of dishes on offer—there's no menu—changes daily depending on what's fresh at local markets, and although the choice is limited, it always includes fish, meat, and vegetarian options. *Haarlemmerstraat 62.* ☎ 020/620-2997. www.lofrestaurant.nl. Fixed-price menu 35€–48€. Dinner Tues–Sun. Tram: 1, 2, 5, 13, or 17 to Martelaarsgracht. Map p 92.

★ **Mamouche** DE PIJP MOROCCAN You'll find innovative trans-Mediterranean cuisine—a blend of North African dishes and French influences—in this gutsy De Pijp restaurant that looks something like a traditional Dutch *eetcafé*. The lamb tagine with prunes, almonds, olives, and lentils is a specialty of the house. *Quellijnstraat 104 (at Marie Heinekenplein).* ☎ 020/670-0736. www.restaurantmamouche.nl. Entrees 16€–24€. Dinner daily. Tram: 16 or 24 to Stadhouderskade. Map p 92.

★★ **Miss Korea Barbecue** DE PIJP KOREAN Another interesting choice among De Pijp's multicultural restaurants, Miss Korea spreads over three buildings and is always packed out with Korean families happily tucking in to their table BBQ of meats and seafood with as many side dishes as they can eat. Despite the crowds, the waitstaff is happy to explain the intricacies of the menu—there's a set price for the main courses, which is halved for kids, and you choose three items per

The Best Dining

person for as many courses as you can stuff down in 2½ hours. *Albert Cuypstraat 66–70.* ☎ *020/679-0606. www.misskorea.nl. Fixed-price menu Mon–Wed 25€, Thur–Sun and public holidays 27€. Dinner daily. Tram: 16 or 24 to Stadhouderskade. Map p 93.*

★ kids **Pancake Bakery** CANAL RING *PANCAKES* A 17th-century canal warehouse is home to this simple eatery where you can sample yummy pancakes with all kinds of toppings and stuffings, from Indonesian chicken to honey, nuts, and whipped cream. *Prinsengracht 191 (at Prinsenstraat).* ☎ *020/625-1333. www.pancake.nl. Pancakes 6€–17€. Lunch and dinner daily. Tram: 13, 14, or 17 to Westermarkt. Map p 93.*

★ **Pasta e Basta** CANAL RING *ITALIAN* This cozy, noisy Italian restaurant has the best opera-singing waiters this side of La Scala. The fantastic antipasti buffet is served

Another trendy Indonesian restauant is Restaurant Blauw (see p 15).

In Amsterdam, a caffe latte (coffee with milk) is called koffie verkeerd. If you order a koffie, you'll probably get black coffee, with sugar and cream on the side.

out of an antique grand piano, and the main courses include a classic spaghetti *vongole* (with clams) and lasagna with pumpkin. There's now a buzzing wine bar, too. *Nieuwe Spiegelstraat 8.* ☎ *020/422-2222. www.pastaebasta.nl. Entrees 14€–28€; fixed-price menus 37€–50€. Dinner daily. Tram: 16 or 24 to Keizersgracht. Map p 93.*

★★ kids **Plancius** PLANTAGE *BRASSERIE* The perfect spot for sitting outside on a sunny day, right opposite the **Artis Royal Zoo** (see p 36). Lunchtime menus offer carefully constructed brasserie-style dishes such as croque monsieur, the a la carte menu serves up organic burgers or steak and fries, and there's a great afternoon tea, too. Overexcited kids impatient to visit the zoo get their own menu and a coloring book to distract them. *Plantage Kerklaan 61.* ☎ *06/2324-4069. www.brasserieplancius.nl. Entrees 13€–19€. Lunch, high tea, and dinner daily. Tram: 9 to Plantage Kerklaan. Map p 93.*

★ **Sama Sebo** MUSEUM DISTRICT *INDONESIAN* This upmarket Indonesian restaurant is decorated with rush mats and batiks and serves a tasty 17-plate rijsttafel (a feast consisting of rice and many accompanying dishes like curried meats, fish, vegetables, and nuts) just a few steps from the **Rijksmuseum** (see p 7). Reservations recommended. *Pieter Cornelisz Hooftstraat 27.* ☎ *020/662-8146.*

www.samasebo.nl. Fixed-price lunch 18€; rijsttafel 32€. Lunch and dinner Mon–Sat. Tram: 2 or 5 to Hobbemastraat. Map p 91.

★★ Soen CANAL RING THAI
A relative newcomer on the block, this stripped-down, wooden-floored Thai is somewhere between a local cafe and sophisticated restaurant. Thai delicacies such as spicy tom yum soup and pad thai noodles are offered with a choice of meats, fish, or vegetarian options and in a variety of chili heats from cowardly to head blasting. The chefs also offer a takeaway delivery service and hampers stuffed full of goodies for picnics on a canal cruise. Prinsengracht 178. ☎ 020/334-2247. soen.thai-food.nl. Entrees 14€–18€. Dinner daily. Tram: 13, 14, or 17 to Westerkerk. Map p 93.

★★ kids Stubbe's Haring OLD CENTER FISH
Raw herring is a Dutch specialty, and there are dozens of haringhuis stands in town. This one, located on a bridge near Centraal Station, is a great spot for raw herring served in a bread roll with pickles and sweet onions. Nieuwe Haarlemmersluis (at Singel). ☎ 020/623-3212. Sandwiches 5.50€. No credit cards. Lunch and dinner daily. Tram: 1, 2, 4, 5, 9, 13, 16, 17, or 24 to Centraal Station. Map p 93.

★ Supperclub OLD CENTER FUSION
Kick back in this ultramodern, blindingly white, hypertrendy restaurant-cum-cocktail bar; stretch out on couches and cushions; and groove along to whatever the DJ is spinning. There's no telling what the chefs (called "food magicians") will whip up—you inform your waiter of any dietary restrictions and wait to see what arrives on your table. The atmosphere, not the food, is the highlight here. Reservations required.

Sample various Indonesian dishes with the rijsttafel at Tempo Doeloe.

Jonge Roelensteeg 21. ☎ 020/344-6400. www.supperclub.com. Entrees 20€; fixed-price menus 69€. Dinner daily. Tram: 1, 2, 4, 5, 9, 13, 14, 16, 17, or 24 to the Dam. Map p 93.

★ Tapas & Crazy Cocktail Bar OLD CENTER SPANISH
This quirky place is decked out like someplace Gaudí designed and is just off Rembrandtplein in the heart of Amsterdam's night-time action. The tapas are not the world's best and it doesn't get going until after 11pm, but when the cocktails start coming across the bar—which is stacked with Spanish brandies and South American tequilas—you can forgive the food as the partying flows out into the streets. Friday and Saturday are salsa nights. Halvemaansteeg 8, off Rembrandtplein. ☎ 020/777-9090. Tapas 6€–9€. Dinner daily. Tram: 4, 9, or 14 to Rembrandtplein. Map p 93.

★★ Tempo Doeloe CANAL RING INDONESIAN
For authentic Indonesian cuisine, this place is hard to beat. You have to ring the bell to get in and it's somewhat cramped. Dishes come in four levels of spiciness and there are three different rijsttafel options, including

The glass-walled terrace at Wilhelmina-Dok.

the 15-plate *stimoelan* and the vegetarian *sayoeran* as well as the sumptuous 25-plate *istemewa*. Other delicious choices include the 12-plate *nasi koening* and all of the vegetarian dishes. Reservations required. *Utrechtsestraat 75, between Prinsengracht and Keizersgracht.* ☎ *020/625-6718. www. tempodoeloerestaurant.nl. Entrees 16€–27€; rijsttafel 30€–38€. Dinner daily. Tram: 4 to Keizersgracht. Map p 93.*

★ **Toscanini** JORDAAN *ITALIAN* This charming eatery has an open kitchen and the unembellished country-style decor is flooded with natural light from skylights during the day. Authentic Italian dishes include fresh pasta (all made on the premises) with hare, seafood risotto, a selection of fresh fish, and lots of chargrilled cuts of meat. *Lindengracht 75.* ☎ *020/623-2813.*

restauranttoscanini.nl. Entrees 14€– 26€. Dinner Mon–Sat. Tram: 3 to Willemsstraat. Map p 93.

★★ **Vinkeles** CANAL RING *FRENCH* This place in the atmospheric setting of a 17th-century almshouse's converted bakery is ultrachic and ultrahip. Top Michelin-starred chef Dennis Kuipers whips up signature dishes such as sea bass with cannabis seed, Iberico ham, and baby squid. Reservations required. *Dylan Hotel, Keizersgracht 384.* ☎ *020/530-2010. www.vinkeles.com. Entrees 34€–60€; fixed-price menus 105€–135€. Dinner Mon–Sat. Tram: 1, 2, 4, 5, 9, 14, 16, or 24 to Spui. Map p 93.*

★★ **Visrestaurant Lucius** OLD CENTER *SEAFOOD* A solid choice for fresh seafood, Lucius offers oysters and lobsters imported from Norway and Canada. The spectacular seafood platter includes mussels, oysters, clams, shrimp, and a half lobster. Reservations recommended. *Spuistraat 247.* ☎ *020/624-1831. www.lucius.nl. Entrees 22€–30€; fixed-price menu 40€; seafood platters for 2 63€–115€. Dinner daily. Tram: 1, 2, 4, 5, 9, 14, 16, or 24 to Spui. Map p 93.*

★ kids **Wilhelmina-Dok** WATERFRONT *CONTINENTAL* With its glass-walled terrace right on the ship channel, this fun cafe-restaurant boasts incredible views of passing boats and the cruise ship terminal on the south shore. Forage the (mostly organic) Mediterranean buffet or choose from the toasties and soups of the day. The views and a children's menu will keep kids happy. *Noordwal 1 (at IJplein).* ☎ *020/632-3701. www.wilhelminadok.nl. Entrees 13€–18€. No cash. Lunch and dinner daily. Ferry: IJpleinveer (IJplein Ferry) to AmsterdamNoord, then walk east a short way along the dike. Map p 93.* ●

Nightlife Best Bets

Best **Place to Sip Wine with the Young & the Beautiful**
★★ Bubbles & Wines, *Nes 37* (p 106)

Best **Place to Drink with the Locals**
★★★ Café Nol, *Westerstraat 109* (p 106)

Friendliest **Gay Bar**
★★ Amstel 54, *Amstel 54* (p 109)

Best **Pub by a Windmill**
★★★ Brouwerij 't IJ, *Funenkade 7* (p 110)

Dance Club **That's Most Worth a Taxi Ride**
★★ Hotel Arena Club, *'s-Gravesandestraat 51* (p 108)

Best **Brown Cafe with a Summer Terrace**
★ Café De Il Prinsen, *Prinsenstraat 27* (p 107)

Best **Place to Dance If You're Looking for Exclusivity**
★★ Jimmy Woo, *Korte Leidsedwarsstraat 18* (p 108)

Most **Hip & Happening Dance Club**
★★ Panama, *Oostelijke Handelskade 4* (p 109)

Best **for Romance**
★ Chocolate Bar, *Eerste Van der Helststraat 62A* (p 107)

Best **for *Gezelligheid* (Dutch Hospitality)**
★★ Café Pollux, *Prins Hendrikkade 121* (p 106)

Best **Lesbian Bar**
★ Vivelavie, *Amstelstraat 7* (p 110)

Best **House-Brewed Beer**
★★ In de Wildeman, *Kolksteeg 3* (p 107)

Best **Place for Clubbing in Industrial Chic**
★★ WesterUnie, *Westergasfabriek, Klönneplein 4–6* (p 109)

Best ***Jenever* Tasting**
★★ Hoppe, *Spui 18–20* (p 107)

Previous page: Sample a Dutch beer at a friendly cafe or bar, like Hoppe.
This page: Heineken is a popular Dutch beer.

De Pijp **Nightlife**

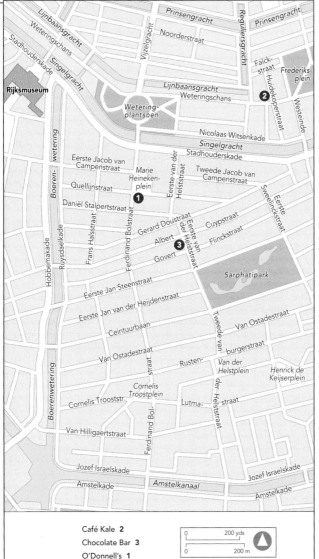

Café Kale **2**
Chocolate Bar **3**
O'Donnell's **1**

| 0 | 200 yds |
| 0 | 200 m |

Central Amsterdam **Nightlife**

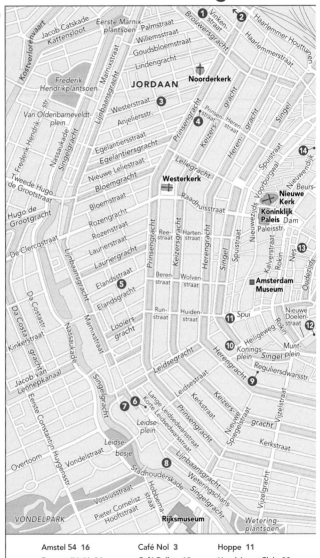

Amstel 54 **16**	Café Nol **3**	Hoppe **11**
Brouwerij 't IJ **21**	Café Pollux **19**	Hotel Arena Club **22**
Bubbles & Wines **13**	De Jaren **12**	In de Wildeman **14**
Café De II Prinsen **4**	Escape **17**	Jimmy Woo **6**

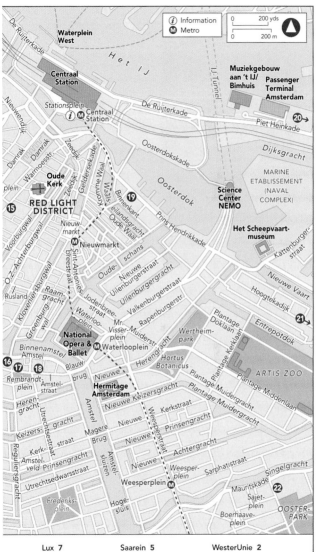

Lux 7
Odeon 10
Panama 20
Paradiso 8

Saarein 5
SoHo Amsterdam 9
Vesper 1
Vivelavie 18

WesterUnie 2
Winston Club 15

Amsterdam Nightlife A to Z

You can meet Amsterdammers at a canal-side cafe or bar.

Bars

★★ Bubbles & Wines OLD
CENTER   Just a few minutes' walk
from the Dam, this fancy champagne and wine bar—all subdued
lighting, dark wood surfaces, and
red tones—serves an extensive roster of champagne and 50 wines by
the glass, alongside snacks of cav-
iar and truffle cheeses. *Nes 37 (at
Pieter Jacobszstraat).* ☎ *020/422-
3318. www.bubblesandwines.com.
Tram: 1, 2, 4, 5, 9, 13, 14, 16, 17, or
24 to the Dam. Map p 104.*

★ Café Kale MUSEUM DISTRICT
Wooden chairs, long red ban-
quettes, and funky chandeliers
draw smart locals and weary tourists fresh from the **Rijksmuseum**
(see p. 7) to sample the draught
and bottled beers and cocktails
while grazing on plates of pasta
and schnitzel. *Weteringschans 267.*
☎ *020/622-6363. www.cafekale.nl.*
*Tram: 7, 4, or 10 to Fredericksplein.
Map p 103.*

★★★ Café Nol JORDAAN   This
cafe has a relaxed bar catering to a
mix of young, cool Jordaaners and
old-timers who have lived in the
neighborhood for ages. The kitsch
interior includes crystal chandeliers,
mirrors, a red carpet, and hanging
potted plants. *Westerstraat 109
(near Noordermarkt).* ☎ *020/624-
5380. www.cafenol-amsterdam.nl.
Tram: 13, 14, or 17 to Westerkerk.
Map p 104.*

★★ Café Pollux OLD CENTER
A real treasure in the Dam area, pri-
marily due to the charismatic and
slightly bonkers owner Frits and his
enigmatic, smiley wife. A simple
menu is served all day and come
evening, there is often live music—
but if not, you can fall back on rock
'n' roll from the 1950s jukebox and
dance around the stripper's pole.
Often open very late, depending
on the mood of the aforemen-
tioned Frits. *Prins Hendrikkade 121.*
☎ *020/624-9521. http://cafepollux.
com. Five-minute walk from Centraal
Station. Map p 104.*

★★ De Jaren OLD CENTER   On
the Binnenamstel waterfront, this
perennial favorite is light and airy,
with a panoramic upper-floor terrace where the young and hip
lounge on sunny days. There's an
enormous bar, a yummy salad buffet, and a traditional English high
tea with scones and clotted cream.
*Nieuwe Doelenstraat 20–22 (at Munt-
plein).* ☎ *020/625-5771. www.cafe-
de-jaren.nl. Tram: 4, 9, 14, 16, or 24
to Muntplein. Map p 104.*

★ Lux LEIDSEPLEIN   Although
the Leidseplein area is very touristy,
1980s throwback Lux draws in a
healthy dose of locals with its chic

Café De II Prinsen is a friendly neighborhood brown cafe.

attitude and probably the rather graphic photos on the walls. Sit on the upper level to watch passing punters doing a double take. *Hotel Weber, Marnixstraat 403 (at Leidsegracht).* ☎ *020/422-1412. www.hotel weber.nl. Tram: 1, 2, 5, 7, or 10 to Leidseplein. Map p 105.*

★★★ **Vesper** JORDAAN   A super-smooth and super-friendly cocktail bar with some wacky and wonderful concoctions, widely regarded as employing the coolest mixologists in Amsterdam. Vesper is also the original home of the alcoholic high tea. *Vinkenstraat 57.* ☎ *020/846-4458. www.vesperbar.nl. Tram: 3 to Haarlemmerplein. Map p 105.*

Brown Cafes

★ **Café De II Prinsen** CANAL RING   The "Two Princes"—in Dutch, De Twee Prinsen—an attractive brown cafe, has mosaic-tiled floors and a wood-muraled ceiling. It's a lovely spot for whiling away summer evenings overlooking Prinsengracht. There's usually a healthy mix of local intellectuals and tourists, from young backpackers to middle-aged professionals. *Prinsenstraat 27.* ☎ *020/624-9722. Tram: 13, 14, or 17 to Westermarkt. Map p 104.*

★ **Chocolate Bar** DE PIJP   A hip hangout with a sparse 1970s retro look, this contemporary brown cafe serves up spiffy cocktails and a really good Thai beef salad. DJs spin great music Thursday through Saturday, and there's a terrace for when the weather's fine. *Eerste Van der Helststraat 62A (at Govert Flinckstraat).* ☎ *020/675-7672. www. chocolate-bar.nl. Tram: 16 or 24 to Albert Cuypstraat. Map p 103.*

★★ **Hoppe** OLD CENTER   An ancient brown cafe dating back to 1670, with a convivial, pubby atmosphere. It's often packed, especially with the after-work crowd, so expect standing room only in the early evenings. It can get rowdy after a few samplings of Dutch *jenevers* (a gin-like liqueur, see p 46). *Spui 18–20.* ☎ *020/420-4420. www. cafe-hoppe.nl. Tram: 1, 2, 4, 5, 9, 14, 16, or 24 to Spui. Map p 104.*

★★ **In de Wildeman** OLD CENTER   First opened in 1690,

Order a colaatje pils (co-la-che pilss) if you want a beer in a small glass, or a bakkie or vaas if you'd like a large.

Brown Cafes

A friendly neighborhood *bruine kroeg* (brown cafe) can be a great place to mix with locals. A lot of Amsterdammers start their day at their favorite brown cafe, have lunch there, and then go back to socialize after work. The brown cafe gets its name because of the centuries-old tobacco stains that have dyed the walls brown. They embody *gezelligheid* (coziness) and evoke a bygone era. Brown cafes' opening hours are somewhere between 8 and 10am and 1 and 3am the following day. They're found all over town and have a fairly standard menu featuring a selection of sandwiches *(broodjes)* made with everything from *Amsterdamse osseworst* (smoked beef sausage) to cheese, vegetables, and salami; *toost* (toasted white bread) with ham and cheese, smoked eel, or beef tartare; and a variety of simple salads.

this historic brown cafe still has the original tiled floor and rows of barrels from when it functioned as a distillery. The bar stocks 18 draft and 250 bottled beers—mostly Dutch, Belgian, or British, and special beers of the month. Its laid-back atmosphere is populated by local ale aficionados who welcome the chance to discuss the brews. *Kolksteeg 3 (at Nieuwendijk).* ☎ *020/638-2348. www.inde wildeman.nl. Tram: 1, 2, 5, 13, or 17 to Nieuwezijds Kolk. Map p 104.*

Dance Clubs
★★ **Escape** REMBRANDTPLEIN
Three dance floors, a great sound system, and an edgy mix of local and international DJs plus party nights make this one of the prime choices for the young and up-for-it. *Rembrandtplein 11.* ☎ *020/622-1111. www.escape.nl. Admission 15€. Tram: 4, 9, or 14 to Rembrandtplein. Map p 104.*

★★ **Hotel Arena Club** OOST
A youngish, well-dressed crowd flocks to this hot club in the ultra-trendy Hotel Arena, where talented DJs keep everybody happy with a mix of music genres and eras. *'s-Gravesandestraat 51 (at Maurits-kade).* ☎ *020/850-2400. www.hotel arena.nl. Admission 6€–12€. Tram: 7 or 10 to Korte 's-Gravesandestraat. Map p 104.*

★★ **Jimmy Woo** LEIDSEPLEIN
An Asian-themed club with a posh clientele who happily sit around quaffing champagne all night. Things don't start to heat up until around 1am, when the music cranks up downstairs and the elegant crowds stalk on to the dance floor. Dress up as the fashion police can be quite picky. *Korte Leidsed-warsstraat 18 (at Leidsestraat).* ☎ *020/626-3150. www.jimmywoo. com. Admission 10€–20€. Tram: 1, 2, 5, 7, or 10 to Leidseplein. Map p 104.*

★ **Odeon** CANAL RING Inside this 17th-century canal house converted into a plush multifunction venue, period ceiling paintings and stucco decor form an incongruous backdrop to the cocktail bar, dance floors, live bands, and electro DJ nights. There's a mini-music festival every Friday night. *Singel 460 (at Koningsplein).* ☎ *020/521-8555.*

Dance the night away at hip nightclub Panama.

www.odeonamsterdam.nl. Admission 10€–15€. Tram: 1, 2, or 5 to Koningsplein. Map p 105.

★★ **Panama** WATERFRONT In a former life, this hip club was a power station, built in 1899. The attractive bar/restaurant in the lobby opens up into the cavernous club, which hosts big-name DJs and weekly special events. This is a see-and-be-seen place for 30- to 40-something professionals who are keen on looking good. *Oostelijke Handelskade 4.* ☎ *020/311-8686. www. panama.nl. Admission 5€–25€. Tram: 10 or 26 to Rietlandpark. Map p 105.*

★ **Paradiso** LEIDSEPLEIN An Amsterdam institution, Paradiso is based in a former church; it's a majestic club with lofty ceilings and high balconies encircling the dance floor. Big-name DJs and theme nights help make this place appealing to a variety of stylish people. *Weteringschans 6–8 (at Max Euweplein).* ☎ *020/626-4521. www. paradiso.nl. Admission 10€–25€. Tram: 1, 2, 5, 7, or 10 to Leidseplein. Map p 105.*

★★ **WesterUnie** WEST Step on the gas for hip-hop, Latin dance, and music festivals at this cavernous venue in the Westergasfabriek (see p 31) west of Centraal Station.

There's also a restaurant and bar with an outdoor terrace. It's often crowded and can be hard to get in if you don't look the part. *Westergasfabriek, Klönneplein 4–6 (at Haarlemmerweg).* ☎ *020/684-8496. www. westerunie.nl. Admission free–75€. Tram: 10 to Van Hallstraat. Map p 105.*

★ **Winston Club** OLD CENTER You'll find a mixed bag of live music, drag shows, sing-alongs, and drum 'n' bass every night of the week in this small, intimate space with a very eclectic, live-and-let-live, quintessentially Amsterdam crowd. *Winston Hotel, Warmoesstraat 129 (behind Beursplein).* ☎ *020/623-1380. www.winston.nl. Admission 7€–15€. Tram: 1, 2, 4, 5, 9, 13, 14, 16, 17, or 24 to the Dam. Map p 105.*

Gay & Lesbian

★★ **Amstel 54** REMBRANDT-PLEIN One of Amsterdam's most venerable gay bars has a definite sense of style, even if it isn't exactly hip. It remains engagingly convivial though, with the occasional sing-alongs, drag competitions, and themed parties. *Amstel 54 (at Halvemaansteeg).* ☎ *020/623-4254. www. facebook.com/pages/Amstel-54/ 263429603773. Tram: 4, 9, or 14 to Rembrandtplein. Map p 104.*

★★ **Saarein** JORDAAN This cafe is a longtime favorite with lesbians, although it now draws a mixed gay crowd. A great brown cafe location in the Jordaan, a pool table, a good range of beer, and a friendly atmosphere make this an appealing choice. *Elandsstraat 119 (at Hazenstraat).* ☎ *020/623-4901. www.saarein.info. Tram: 7 or 17 to Elandsgracht. Map p 105.*

★ **SoHo Amsterdam** OLD CENTER The city's quintessential gay venue is a typical pub during the week but hits party time at the weekend. Nothing really gets going until after 11pm, and there are DJ nights and themed parties right in the heart of Amsterdam's gay area. *Reguliersdwarsstraat 36 (behind the Flower Market).* ☎ *020/638-5700. soho-amsterdam.com. Tram: 1, 2, or 5 to Koningsplein. Map p 105.*

★ **Vivelavie** REMBRANDTPLEIN Open for more than 30 years, this cafe is the place for lesbians in Amsterdam. There are weekend DJ nights and dancing to camp mainstream chart hits. *Amstelstraat 7 (off Rembrandtplein).* ☎ *020/624-0114. www.vivelavie.net. Tram: 4, 9, or 14 to Rembrandtplein. Map p 105.*

Pubs

★★★ **Brouwerij 't IJ** PLANTAGE Ideal for a sunny afternoon, this pub has a gorgeous terrace overlooking the IJ waterway. All the beers are made in the onsite brewery next to the landmark De Gooyer Windmill; Belgian-style *tripels* and blondes are specialties. *Funenkade 7.* ☎ *020/528-6237. www.brouwerijhetij.nl. Tram: 10 to Hoogte Kadijk. Map p 104.*

★★ **O'Donnell's** DE PIJP This neighborhood Irish pub pulls in many of the young, up-and-coming professionals who live in De Pijp. It's a boisterous place where the bartenders are Irish, the Guinness is poured right, and there are vast screens for expats to watch the big sports matches. *Ferdinand Bolstraat 5 (at Marie Heinekenplein).* ☎ *020/676-7786. www.odonnells amsterdam.nl. Tram: 16 or 24 to Stadhouderskade. Map p 103.* ●

Soft Drugs Tolerance

Amsterdam's reputation as a party town is due in part to its *tolerance* toward soft drugs. But the practice is technically illegal. Whereas it's fine to carry 5 grams (⅙ oz.) for personal use, it's not fine to buy it anywhere other than in a coffee shop (see p 44). This is a licensed and controlled venue where you can purchase marijuana or hashish, and can sit and smoke all day if you choose to. Although around 200 coffee shops still exist in Amsterdam, many have been closed down since 2010 as the civic leaders have tried to clean up the city's act (see p 45). There was even talk back in 2012 of introducing an ID system for coffee shop users that would have banned overseas tourists from utilizing them, but this was rather cynically vetoed as financially unviable for the city. However, it is still illegal to smoke dope in the streets, to buy drugs in the streets, and to buy drugs at all if you are under 18. And don't be tempted to take any drugs out of the country with you.

Arts & Entertainment Best Bets

Best **Place for Laughing the Night Away**
★ Boom Chicago, *Rozengracht 117* (p 116)

Best **Last-Minute Ticket Offers**
★★ Last Minute Ticket Shop, *Leidseplein 26* (p 120)

Best **for Controversial Movies**
★★ De Balie, *Kleine-Gartmanplantsoen 10 (p 118)*

Best **Acoustics**
★★★ Concertgebouw, *Concertgebouwplein 2–6 (p 116)*

Best **Contemporary Concert Space**
★ Heineken Music Hall, *ArenA Boulevard 590 (p 116)*

Best **for Opera**
★★★ Dutch National Opera & Ballet, *Amstel 3 (p 117)*

Best **for Gay & Lesbian Plays**
★ Melkweg, *Lijnbaansgracht 234A* (p 120)

Best **for Lavish Musicals**
★★★ Carré, *Amstel 115–125* (p 119)

Best **for Summer Beachtime Fun**
★★★ Blijburg aan Zee, *Muiderlaan 1001 (p 119)*

Best **for Modern Dutch Theater**
★★ Stadsschouwburg, *Leidseplein 26 (p 120)*

Best **Blues Venue**
★★ Maloe Melo, *Lijnbaansgracht 163 (p 118)*

Best **for Experimental Music**
★★ Muziekgebouw aan 't IJ, *Piet Heinkade 1 (p 117)*

Best **Free Open-air Concerts**
★★★ Vondelpark Openluchttheater, *Vondelpark (p 117)*

Previous page: Check out a concert at the Muziekgebouw aan 't IJ, the hub of contemporary and experimental music in Amsterdam. This page: Concertgebouw, the home of the Royal Concertgebouw Orchestra.

Museum District **A&E**

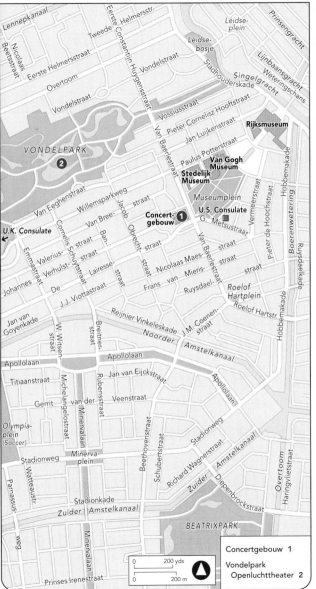

Concertgebouw **1**

Vondelpark
  Openluchttheater **2**

Central Amsterdam **A&E**

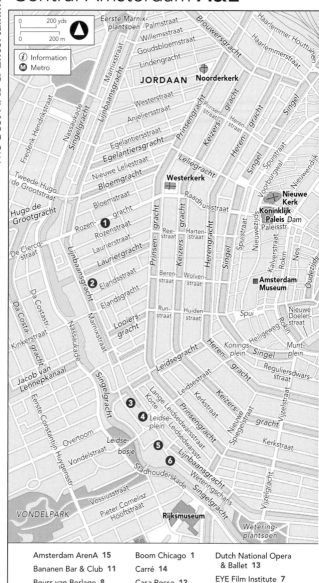

	200 yds
0	200 m

ⓘ Information
Ⓜ Metro

Eerste Marnix-plantsoen
Palmstraat
Willemsstraat
Brouwersgracht
Haarlemmer Houttuinen
Haarlemmerstraat
Goudsbloemstraat
Lindengracht
Marnixstraat
JORDAAN **Noorderkerk**
Singel
Prinsengracht
Westerstraat
Anjeliersstraat
Keizersgracht
Herengracht
Singel
Egelantiersstraat
Egelantiersgracht
Nieuwe Leliestraat
Leliegracht
Westerkerk
Frederik Hendrikstraat
Nassaukade
Singelgracht
Lijnbaansgracht
Bloemgracht
Raadhuisstraat
Nieuwe
Kerk
Tweede Hugo de Grootstraat
Bloemstraat
Reestraat
Hartenstraat
Herengracht
Prinsengracht
Keizersgracht
Singel
Spuistraat
Voorburgwal
Nieuwendijk
Koninklijk
Paleis Dam
Paleisstr.
Hugo de Grootgracht
Rozen-gracht
Rozenstraat
Laurierstraat
Lauriergracht
Nieuwezijds
Kalverstraat
Rokin
De Clercqstraat
Berenstraat
Wolvenstraat
Amsterdam
Museum
Nes
Oudezijds
Da Costakade
Lijnbaansgracht
Elandsstraat
Elandsgracht
Runstraat
Huidenstraat
Spui
Nieuwe Doelenstraat
Kinkerstraat
Marnixstraat
Looiersgracht
Leidsegracht
Herengracht
Koningsplein
Heiligeweg
Rokin
Muntplein
Jacob van Lennepkanaal
Nassaukade
Leidsestraat
Prinsengracht
Keizersgracht
Singel
Reguliersdwarsstraat
Eerste Constantijn Huygensstr.
Singelgracht
Lange Leidsedwarsstr.
Korte Leidsedwarsstr.
Leidseplein
Nieuwe Spiegelstraat
Kerkstraat
Vijzelstraat
Overtoom
Vondelstraat
Leidsebosje
Lijnbaansgracht
Weteringschans
Vijzelgracht
Vossiusstraat
Stadhouderskade
Singelgracht
VONDELPARK
Pieter Cornelisz Hooftstraat
Rijksmuseum
Weteringplantsoen

Amsterdam ArenA **15**	Boom Chicago **1**	Dutch National Opera
Bananen Bar & Club **11**	Carré **14**	& Ballet **13**
Beurs van Berlage **8**	Casa Rosso **12**	EYE Film Institute **7**
Bimhuis **10**	De Balie **5**	Heineken Music Hall **16**

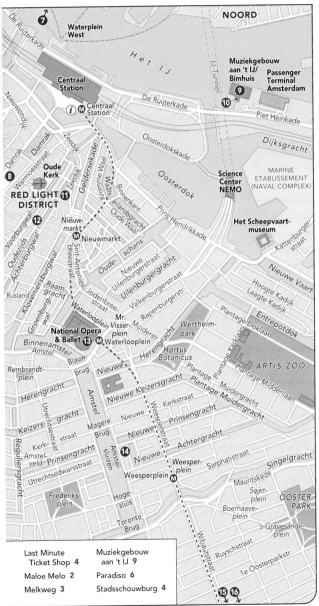

NOORD

Waterplein
West

Het IJ

Centraal
Station

Muziekgebouw
aan 't IJ/
Bimhuis

Passenger
Terminal
Amsterdam

i Centraal
Station

De Ruijterkade

Piet Heinkade

Oosterdokskade

Dijksgracht

Oosterdok

MARINE
ETABLISSEMENT
(NAVAL COMPLEX)

Science
Center
NEMO

Oude
Kerk

RED LIGHT
DISTRICT

Prins Hendrikkade

Het Scheepvaart-
museum

Binnenkant
Eilandsgracht
Oude Waal

Nieuw-
markt

Nieuwmarkt

Oude schans

Nieuwe
Uilenburgerstraat

Uilenburgergracht

Hoogte Kadijk
Laagte Kadijk

Nieuwe Vaart

Sint-Antonies-
breestraat

Jodenbree-
straat

Valkenburgerstraat

Entrepotdok

Rapenburgerstr.

Plantage
Doklaan

Raam-
gracht

Waterlooplein

Mr.
Visser-
plein

Wertheim-
park

National Opera
& Ballet

Waterlooplein

Herengracht

Plantage Kerklaan

ARTIS ZOO

Binnenamstel
Amstel

Rembrandt-
plein

Blauw-
brug

Nieuwe

Hortus
Botanicus

Plantage Middenlaan

Herengracht

Nieuwe Keizersgracht

Plantage Muidergracht

Keizers- gracht

Nieuwe

Kerkstraat

Prinsengracht

Magere
Brug

Nieuwe

Achtergracht

Singelgracht

Amstel-
sluizen

Kerk-
straat

Amstel-
veld

Prinsengracht

Nieuwe

Weesperstraat

Sarphatistraat

Mauritskade

OOSTER-
PARK

Utrechtsedwarsstraat

Weesperplein

Weesper-
plein

Sajet-
plein

Boerhaave-
plein

's-Gravesande-
plein

Frederiks-
plein

Hoge-
sluis

Toronto
Brug

Ruyschstraat

1e Oosterparkstr.

Wibautstraat

Last Minute Ticket Shop 4	Muziekgebouw aan 't IJ 9
Maloe Melo 2	Paradiso 6
Melkweg 3	Stadsschouwburg 4

Arts & Entertainment A to Z

An improv performance at Boom Chicago.

Classical Music

★ Beurs van Berlage OLD

CENTER The former home of the Amsterdam Stock Exchange, an architectural marvel from 1903 designed by Hendrik Berlage, is now an exhibition center and sometime concert venue with two halls hosting classical concerts and rock festivals. *Beursplein 1 (at the Dam).* ☎ *020/531-3355. www.beurs vanberlage.nl. Tickets start at 10€. Tram: 1, 2, 4, 5, 9, 13, 14, 16, 17, or 24 to the Dam. Map p 114.*

★★★ Concertgebouw MUSEUM

DISTRICT The home of the Royal Concertgebouw Orchestra, the Netherlands Philharmonic, and the Netherlands Chamber Orchestra first opened its doors in 1888 and is still touted as one of the most acoustically perfect concert halls in Europe. The world's finest conductors, orchestras, ensembles, and soloists regularly perform here. There are two halls: the main auditorium and a recital hall, which hosts smaller concerts. Free concerts every Wednesday at 12:30pm. *Concertgebouwplein 2–6 (at Museumplein).* ☎ *0900/671-8345. www.concertgebouw.nl. Tickets 18€–70€. Tram: 3, 5, 12, 16, or 24 to Museumplein. Map p 113.*

Comedy Theater

★ Boom Chicago LEIDSEPLEIN

Amsterdam's premier comedy theater has been going strong since 1993. The partly scripted, partly improvised humor takes aim at life in Amsterdam, the Dutch, tourists, and any other convenient target. Most performances are in English. *Rozengracht 117.* ☎ *0900/266-6244. www.boomchicago.nl. Tickets 10€–27€. Tram: 10 to Rozengracht or 13, 14, or 17 to Marnixstraat. Map p 114.*

Concerts

★ Amsterdam ArenA ZUIDOOST

From sports (soccer, mostly, at the home of Ajax) to big-name rock concerts and jazz festivals, the city's biggest events take place at this giant arena, located in southeast Amsterdam. *ArenA Boulevard 1 (at Amsterdam ArenA).* ☎ *020/311-1333. www.amsterdamarena.nl. Tickets 18€–65€. Metro: Line 54 to Bijlmer ArenA. Map p 114.*

★ Heineken Music Hall ZUI-

DOOST Near the Amsterdam ArenA, this smaller venue hosts more intimate concerts and events. Recent performers have included Katy Perry, Jack White, and dog whisperer Cesar Millan. *ArenA Boulevard 590.* ☎ *0900/687-4242.*

www.heineken-music-hall.nl. Tickets
38€–65€. Metro: Line 54 to Bijlmer
ArenA. Map p 114.

★★ Muziekgebouw aan 't IJ
WATERFRONT   This spectacular
modern glass construction, located
on the IJ waterfront east of Centraal
Station, is the hub of contemporary
and experimental music in Amsterdam. Top local and international
musicians perform here. The jazz
club **Bimhuis** (see p 118) is adjacent. *Piet Heinkade 1.* ☎ *020/788-
2000. www.muziekgebouw.nl. Tickets
10€–28€. Tram: 26 to Muziekgebouw
Bimhuis. Map p 115.*

★ Paradiso LEIDSEPLEIN   This
former church is a multipurpose
venue, great for dance events
(Thurs–Sun; see p 109), and it doubles as a concert venue for big-
name artists. The Rolling Stones,
Arcade Fire, Robbie Williams, and
Adele have all played here. *Weteringschans 6–8 (at Max Euweplein).*
☎ *020/626-4521. www.paradiso.nl.
Concert tickets 10€–100€. Tram: 1, 2,
5, 7, or 10 to Leidseplein. Map p 115.*

★★★ Vondelpark Openlucht-
theater MUSEUM DISTRICT   This
open-air venue comes to life on certain nights from May through August,
when pop, rock, Latin, or classical
artists give free concerts in the midst

Muziekgebouw aan 't IJ.

of peaceful, green Vondelpark (see
p 15). Bring a picnic and enjoy an
enchanting evening under the stars.
Vondelpark (at Grote Vijver pond).
☎ *020/428-3360. www.openlucht
theater.nl. Free admission. Tram: 1, 2,
5, 7, or 10 to Leidseplein. Map p 113.*

Dance & Opera
★★★ Dutch National Opera
& Ballet WATERLOOPLEIN   One
of the city's stellar performance
venues, this place has a superbly
equipped 1,600-seat auditorium
and is the home base of both the
highly regarded Dutch National

Vondelpark Openluchttheater.

Members of the Dutch National Opera & Ballet perform Prokofiev's L'amour des trois oranges.

Opera and the National Ballet. The acclaimed Netherlands Dance Theater, based in The Hague, also performs here regularly. *Amstel 3. ☎ 020/625-5455. www.het-muziek theater.nl. Tickets 15€–154€. Tram: 9 or 14 to Waterlooplein. Map p 114.*

Film

★★ **De Balie** LEIDSEPLEIN This all-purpose cultural center has an eclectic calendar of workshops, lectures, and film festivals as well as a restaurant. You can see controversial and award-winning features and documentaries and lots of interesting movies from around the world that don't make it to mainstream theaters. *Kleine-Gartmanplantsoen 10 (at Max Euweplein). ☎ 020/553-5100. www.debalie.nl. Movie tickets 9€–10€; lectures free–10€. Tram: 1, 2, 5, 7, or 10 to Leidseplein. Map p 114.*

★★★ **EYE Film Institute** WATERFRONT Much more than a film museum, this art cinema moved in 2012 from its old location in Vondelpark to a strikingly modern building in Amsterdam-Noord (see p 29). The new complex houses four movie theaters, exhibitions, a store, and a restaurant. EYE does not accept cash. *IJpromenade 1. ☎ 020/589-1400. www.eyefilm.nl. Movie tickets 10€ adults, 7.50€ kids 10 and under. Free ferry: behind Centraal Station to Buiksloterwegveer. Map p 114.*

Jazz

★ **Bimhuis** WATERFRONT Next door to the Muziekgebouw aan 't IJ (see p 117), this is the city's premier jazz, blues, and improvisational venue. *Piet Heinkade 3. ☎ 020/788-2188. bimhuis.com. Tickets free–30€. Tram: 26 to Muziekgebouw Bimhuis. Map p 114.*

★★ **Maloe Melo** JORDAAN This small club presents live music every night, interspersed with evenings of jazz and country, plus DJs sometimes on the weekend. Sunday through Thursday sees jam sessions kicking off at 11pm; these are free. *Lijnbaansgracht 163 (at Lauriergracht). ☎ 020/420-4592. www. maloemelo.nl. Cover 5€. Tram: 7, 10, or 17 to Elandsgracht. Map p 115.*

Sex Shows

★ **Bananen Bar & Club** OLD CENTER Bananas are the featured props in the nightly sex shows, where the audiences tend toward hormone-driven youths. Upstairs, pole dancers gyrate lethargically to pop music in the dance club. *Oudezijds Achterburgwal 37 (at Molensteeg). ☎ 020/627-8954. www.bananenbar.nl. Cover: 60€ for an hour, including all drinks; club 25€. Metro: Nieuwmarkt. Map p 114.*

★ **Casa Rosso** OLD CENTER In its own words, Casa Rosso puts on

Summertime City Beaches

Yes, that's right, beaches. Amsterdam has no natural beaches of its own, so it decided to create some. And what's even better is that admission is free, both to facilities and daily entertainment programs. **Blijburg aan Zee** ★★★ is out at IJburg Zuid (Muiderlaan 1001; ☎ 020/416-0330; www.blijburg.nl; tram 26) in the eastern suburbs, backed by a man-made sandy strip with a bohemian vibe, campfires, and late-night summertime clubbing. Party central for the young and hip of the city is **Strand West** ★ at Stavangerweg 900 (☎ 020/682-6310; www.strand-west.nl), just north of the Westerpark and 15 minutes from Centraal Station by buses 22 or 48; here you'll find parasols, volleyball, beach bars, night-time DJs, and dance parties. Sophisticated **Strandzuid** ★★ at Europaplein 22 (☎ 020/639-2589; www.strand-zuid.nl) is the preserve of a rather more mature clientele, with a restaurant, chill-out lounge, and cocktail bar on the wooden boardwalk. It's south of De Pijp; catch tram 4.

"one of the most superior erotic shows in the world, with a tremendous choreography and a high-level cast." You may not describe it in this way, but this live sex show joint is very popular with throngs of visiting men. *Oudezijds Achterburgwal 106–108 (at Stoofsteeg).* ☎ *020/627-8954. www.casarosso.nl. Cover 40€–50€, including 2 drinks. Tram: 1, 2, 4, 5, 9, 13, 14, 16, 17, or 24 to the Dam. Map p 114.*

Theater
★★★ Carré OOST   This big, plush theater used to be a circus arena; now a circus performs here only over Christmas. The theater hosts the most lavish Dutch-language (and some English) productions of opera, modern dance, and ballet, as well as best-selling shows such as *War Horse.* Big-name acts (Neil Finn, Glenn Miller Orchestra) also perform here. *Amstel 115–125 (at Nieuwe Prinsengracht).*

Jazz musicians performing at Bimhuis.

Last-Minute Tickets

Although the reception staff at most hotels can help you book tickets, the most convenient outlet in the city is **I amsterdam's Last Minute Ticket Shop** ★★ in the Stadsschouwburg at Leidseplein 26 (www.lastminuteticketshop.nl; Mon–Sat 10am–6pm; tram: 1, 2, 5, 7, or 10), which sells half-price tickets for same-day performances after 10am every morning. You can buy tickets for any venue in town and pick up schedules for Amsterdam's cultural events. Two other branches are at the Amsterdam Public Library at Oosterdokskade 143 (Mon–Fri 10am–7:30pm, Sat–Sun 10am–6pm) and the Amsterdam Tourist Office at Stationsplein 10 outside Centraal Station (Sat 9am–5pm, Sun 10am–5pm). There's a nominal booking charge of 2€ to 5€ for all tickets. To find out what's happening on Amsterdam's cultural scene, the I amsterdam website (www.iamsterdam.com) is an informative starting point.

☎ 0900/252-5255. carre.nl. Tickets 5€–140€. Tram: 7 or 10 to Weesperplein. Map p 114.

★ **Melkweg** LEIDSEPLEIN This large contemporary multidimensional venue includes a theater, cinema, concert hall, photo gallery, and exhibition space. Its theater tends to showcase new groups, both international and local (most performances are in Dutch), with emphasis on experimentalism. *Lijnbaansgracht 234A (at Leidsegracht).* ☎ 020/531-8181. www.melkweg.nl.

Tickets free–25€. Tram: 1, 2, 5, 7, or 10 to Leidseplein. Map p 115.

★★ **Stadsschouwburg** LEIDSEPLEIN This 950-seat municipal theater is Amsterdam's main venue for mainstream Dutch theater. Opera and ballet performances are occasionally staged, as are classic and modern plays in English. The Last Minute Ticket Shop is on the ground floor. *Leidseplein 26.* ☎ 020/624-2311. www.ssba.nl. Tickets 9€–38€. Tram: 1, 2, 5, 7, or 10 to Leidseplein. Map p 115. ●

A performance at the Carré theater.

Lodging **Best Bets**

Best **Canal House Hotel**
★★ Estheréa $$$–$$$$ *Singel 303–309 (p 129)*

Best **for Bicycle Lovers**
★ Bicycle Hotel Amsterdam $–$$ *Van Ostadestraat 123 (p 127)*

Best **for John Lennon Fans**
★ Hilton Amsterdam $$$$–$$$$$ *Apollolaan 138 (p 130)*

Best **for Techies**
★ citizenM Amsterdam City $–$$ *Prinses Irenestraat 30 (p 127)*

Best **for Business Travelers**
★★ Renaissance Amsterdam $$$$–$$$$$ *Kattengat 1 (p 133)*

Best **When Money Is No Object**
★★ Seven One Seven $$$$$ *Prinsengracht 717 (p 134)*

Best **for Affordable Minimalist Design**
★★ Arena $$–$$$ *'s-Gravesandestraat 51 (p 127)*

Best **Boutique Hotel**
★★★ The Dylan $$$$$ *Keizersgracht 384 (p 129)*

Best **Location for Families**
★ Hampshire Hotel Lancaster Amsterdam $$–$$$ *Plantage Middenlaan 48 (p 129)*

Best **for Young Party Animals**
★★ Winston $$ *Warmoesstraat 129 (p 134)*

Best **Place to Call Home**
★★★ Seven Bridges $$–$$$ *Reguliersgracht 31 (p 134)*

Best **Romantic Getaway**
★★★ Pulitzer $$$$$ *Prinsengracht 315–331 (p 132)*

Best **Minimalist Interior Design**
★★ Lloyd Hotel & Cultural Embassy $–$$$$$ *Oostelijke Handelskade 34 (p 130)*

Best **Affordable Hotel with Elegant Rooms**
★ Piet Hein $–$$$$ *Vossiusstraat 52–53 (p 132)*

Best **for Green Credentials**
★★ Conscious Hotel Vondelpark $–$$$ *Overtoom 519 (p 128)*

Best **for Cultivating the Mental Faculties**
★★ Sandton Hotel De Filosoof $$–$$$ *Anna van den Vondelstraat 6 (p 133)*

Previous page: A suite at the Hotel Estheréa.
This page: A deluxe suite at the Ambassade Hotel.

Museum District **Lodging**

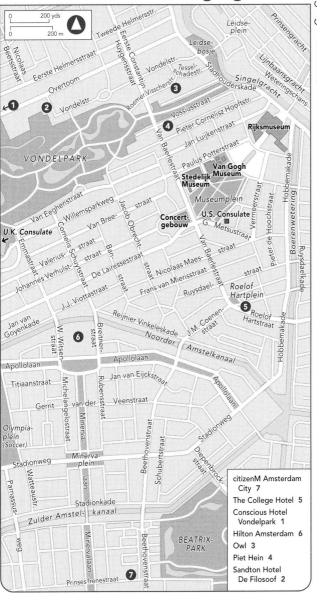

0 200 yds
0 200 m

Tweede Helmersstr.
Eerste Helmersstraat
Overtoom
Nicolaas Beetsstraat
Eerste Constantijn Huygensstraat
Vondelstr.
Roemer Visscherst.
Tessel-schadestr.
Vondelstr.
Sadhouderskade
Leidse-bosje
Leidse-plein
Prinsengracht
Lijnbaansgracht
Weteringschans
Singelgracht

Vossiusstraat
Pieter Cornelisz Hooftstr.
Van Baerlestraat
Jan Luijkenstraat
Paulus Potterstraat
Rijksmuseum
Hobbemakade

VONDELPARK

Van Eeghenstraat
Willemsparkweg
Jacob Obrecht- straat
Van Gogh Museum
Stedelijk Museum
Museumplein
Vermeerstraat
Pieter de Hoochstraat
Boerenwetering
Ruysdaelkade

U.K. Consulate
Cornelis Schuytstraat
Van Bree- straat
Concert-gebouw
U.S. Consulate
G. Metsustraat
Van Baerlestraat
Emmastraat
Valerius- straat
Ban- straat
De Lairessestraat
Nicolaas Maes- straat
Johannes Verhulst-
J.J. Viottastraat
Frans van Mierisstraat
Ruysdael-
straat
Roelof Hartplein
Roelof Hartstraat
Hobbemakade

Jan van Goyenkade
W.-Witsen straat
Breitner-straat
Reijnier Vinkeleskade
Noorder
J.M.-Coenen-straat
Amstelkanaal

Apollolaan
Apollolaan
Jan van Eijckstraat
Veenstraat
Apollolaan

Titiaanstraat
Michelangelostraat
Rubensstraat
Beethovenstraat
Schubertstraat
Stadionweg
Diepenbrock-straat

Gerrit
van der Minerva-

Olympia-plein (Soccer)
Stadionweg
Minerva-plein
Minervalaan

Watteaustr.
Parnassus-weg
Stadionkade
Zuider Amstel- kanaal
Minervalaan
Beethovenstraat

BEATRIX-PARK

Prinses Irenestraat

citizenM Amsterdam
  City **7**
The College Hotel **5**
Conscious Hotel
  Vondelpark **1**
Hilton Amsterdam **6**
Owl **3**
Piet Hein **4**
Sandton Hotel
  De Filosoof **2**

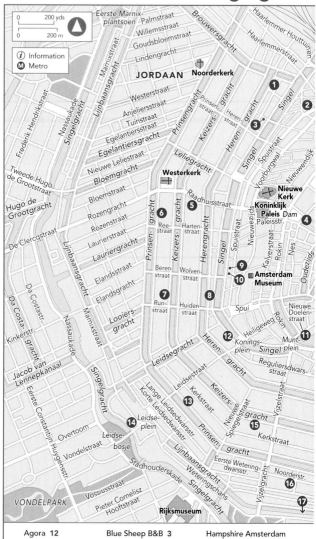

Central Amsterdam **Lodging**

Agora **12**
Ambassade Hotel **8**
Amstel Botel **26**
Arena **21**
Bicycle Hotel
   Amsterdam **17**

Blue Sheep B&B **3**
The Bridge Hotel **20**
chic&basic Amsterdam **1**
Clemens Amsterdam **5**
The Dylan **7**
Estheréa **10**

Hampshire Amsterdam
   American Hotel **14**
Hampshire Hotel
   Lancaster Amsterdam **22**
Hoksbergen **9**
Hotel de l'Europe **11**

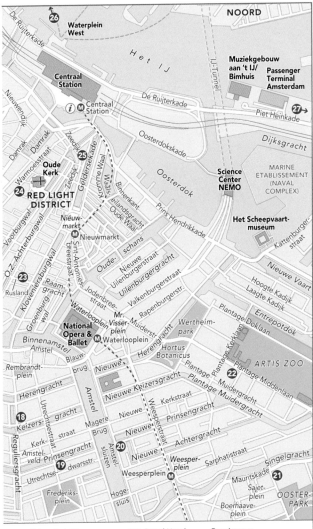

Keizershof **15**

Lloyd Hotel & Cultural
Embassy **27**

Mauro Mansion **25**

Mercure Amsterdam
Arthur Frommer **16**

NH Grand Hotel
Krasnapolsky **4**

Prinsenhof **19**

Pulitzer **6**

Radisson Blu **23**

Renaissance
Amsterdam **2**

Seven Bridges **18**

Seven One Seven **13**

Winston **24**

Amsterdam Hotels A to Z

The Hotel Agora.

★ **Agora** CANAL RING Great location and friendly service make this small hotel a good value. Rooms are fairly small and quite old-fashioned, outfitted with mahogany and antiques. Those overlooking the canal can be somewhat noisy, so if you're a light sleeper ask for a room in back, with views of a leafy garden. There's no elevator. *Singel 462 (at Koningsplein).*

☎ 020/627-2200. www.hotelagora. nl. 16 units. Doubles 80€–180€ w/ breakfast. Free WiFi. Tram: 1, 2, or 5 to Koningsplein. Map p 124.

★★ **Ambassade Hotel** CANAL RING Ten elegant 17th- and 18th-century canal houses have been renovated to create this perfectly located gem. Individually decorated rooms are furnished in Louis XV and XVI styles. Five lusciously appointed suites and one apartment are also available. Not all rooms are accessible by elevator. *Herengracht 341 (at Huidenstraat).* ☎ 020/555-0222. www.ambassade-hotel.nl. 58 units. Doubles 186€–225€ w/breakfast. Free WiFi. Tram: 1, 2, or 5 to Spui. Map p 124.

★ **Amstel Botel** WATERFRONT Where better to experience a city-on-the-water than on a boat hotel? This retired inland waterways cruise boat, moored permanently to a dock on the IJ waterway northwest of Centraal Station, has cabins on four decks. It's hugely popular largely because of that extra thrill of sleeping on the water, so book well in advance. The rooms are no great shakes but functional and spotless. *NDSM-Pier 3 (north shore of the IJ).* ☎ 020/626-4247. www.amstelbotel.nl.

Experience a city-on-the-water boat hotel at Amstel Botel.

175 units. Doubles 79€ w/breakfast. Free WiFi. Boat: NDSM Ferry from Centraal Station (or a free shuttle bus at night when the ferry's not running). Map p 124.

★★ **Arena** OOST   Formerly an orphanage dating to 1890, the Arena is now a stylish hotel catering mostly to European yuppies who love the minimalistic modern rooms and suites, each individually decorated by up-and-coming Dutch designers. There's a smart bar and eatery, a cute little terrace bar, and a hot nightclub in the former orphanage chapel (see p 108). 's-Gravesandestraat 51 (at Mauritskade). ☎ 020/850-2400. www. hotelarena.nl. 127 units. Doubles 99€–209€ w/breakfast. Free WiFi. Tram: 7 or 10 to Korte 's-Gravesandestraat. Map p 124.

★ **Bicycle Hotel Amsterdam** DE PIJP   Located a few blocks from the popular **Albert Cuypmarkt** (see p 75), this eco-friendly hotel caters to visitors who wish to explore Amsterdam on bicycles. You can rent bikes for 7.50€ per day and stable your trusty steed indoors. The guest rooms have plain but comfortable modern furnishings; some have kitchenettes and small balconies; and there are large rooms for families. There's no elevator and payment is preferred in cash. Van Ostadestraat 123 (off Ferdinand Bolstraat). ☎ 020/679-3452. www.bicyclehotel.com. 16 units. Doubles 50€–120€ w/breakfast. Free WiFi. Tram: 16 to Albert Cuypstraat. Map p 124.

★★ **Blue Sheep B&B** OLD CENTER   This stylish, family-run gem is in a gorgeous canal house on a car-free street. There's no elevator and the pristine bathrooms are shared, but contemporary fixtures, classy decor, airy rooms, and a standout mega-breakfast all make this place a great choice. And the owners must be doing something right as their empire has grown to incorporate a selection of beautifully appointed apartments and suites suitable for romantic couples or families with young kids—but be warned, several choices have very steep stairs. Korsjespoortsteeg 3. ☎ 06/2962-3499. www.theblue sheep.net. 13 units. Doubles 119€–249€ w/breakfast. Free WiFi. Walk from Centraal Station. Map p 124.

★ **The Bridge Hotel** OOST   The riverfront location and large, simply furnished, but comfortable rooms make this hotel a great value. Two airy and spacious apartments with picture windows are great for families. The full Dutch breakfast served every morning is a nice touch. Amstel 107–111 (near Carré). ☎ 020/623-7068. www.thebridgehotel.nl. 48 units. Doubles 129€–179€ w/breakfast. Free WiFi. Tram: 7 or 10 to Weesperplein. Map p 124.

★ **chic&basic Amsterdam** CANAL RING   Another example of the new winds blowing through the Amsterdam hotel world, this boutique hotel is tucked away behind a canal-house facade. The compact rooms are gaily decorated with homey touches like patchwork quilts and wackily upholstered comfy chairs, while the public spaces in the hotel are smooth and contemporary. Best of all is the light-filled loft apartment with glorious views across the canal—but there's no elevator. Herengracht 13–19 (at Negen Straatjes). ☎ 020/522-2345. www.chicandbasic.com. 28 units. Doubles 135€–190€ w/breakfast. Free WiFi. Tram: 13, 14, or 17 to Westerkerk. Map p 124.

★ **citizenM Amsterdam City** NIEUW ZUID   With an ultramodern design, high-tech touch-screen remotes, and free WiFi, this could be the perfect Amsterdam abode for mobile citizens of the world. A

One of the ultramodern rooms at citizenM Amsterdam City.

fast tram connection to the center of town compensates for a location in the business-oriented World Trade Center zone. *Prinses Irenestraat 30 (at Beethovenstraat).* ☎ *020/811-7090. www.citizenm. com/amsterdam-city. 215 units. Doubles 79€–159€. Free WiFi. Tram: 5 to Prinses Irenestraat. Map p 123.*

★ Clemens Amsterdam

JORDAAN This recently upgraded hotel is comfortable and friendly and in pole position near many of the city's main attractions. All of the fairly spacious rooms are bright, clean, and homey, and some have tiny balconies facing the Westerkerk. The hotel occupies four floors in a steep-staired building, and there's no elevator. *Raadhuisstraat 39 (close to the Anne Frank Huis).* ☎ *020/ 624-6089. www.clemenshotel.nl. 14 units. Doubles 85€–100€ w/breakfast. Free WiFi. Tram: 13, 14, or 17 to Westerkerk. Map p 124.*

★★ The College Hotel MUSEUM

DISTRICT This glammy, modern boutique hotel is housed in a former school building (hence the name) just a short walk from the major museums. Expect to see plenty of trendy 30-something European professionals here. *Roelof Hartstraat 1 (at Van Baerlestraat).* ☎ *020/571-1511. www.thecollege hotel.com. 40 units. Doubles 125€– 230€. Free WiFi. Tram: 3, 5, 12, or 24 to Roelof Hartplein. Map p 123.*

★★ Conscious Hotel Vondel-

park VONDELPARK This new arrival on the Dutch accommodation scene shouts its green credibility throughout, with living plant walls, eco-roofs, and green energy. It's run by a young, handsome, and very cool staff who go the whole hog to help and make recommendations. They let their collective hair down on the weekends when

At Conscious Hotel Vondelpark, you'll find a cozy bar decorated with a plant wall where organic drinks and homemade bites are served.

The Dylan Thomas suite at the Dylan Hotel.

every night is party night, with music and dancing in the bar. Bedrooms are compact and wittily decorated; the breakfast bar an organic delight. A sister hotel is near Museumplein. *Overtoom 519.* ☎ *020/820-3333. www.conscious hotels.com. 81 units. Doubles 89€– 175€. Free WiFi. Tram: 1 to Overtoomsesluis. Map p 123.*

★★★ **The Dylan** CANAL RING Amsterdam's swankiest boutique hotel is set in a 17th-century building on one of the city's most scenic canals. Modern elegance reigns here—many rooms have four-poster beds and spacious bathrooms. Each room is individually decorated with rich fabrics and bold colors. *Keizersgracht 384 (at Runstraat).* ☎ *020/530-2010. dylan amsterdam.com. 39 units. Doubles 350€–795€ w/breakfast. Free WiFi. Tram: 1, 2, or 5 to Spui. Map p 124.*

★★ **Estheréa** CANAL RING This elegant boutique hotel, which is built within a group of neighboring 17th-century canal houses, has been owned by the same family since it opened. In the 1940s, the proprietors installed wood paneling, crystal chandeliers, and other structural additions. Wood bedsteads and dresser-desks lend luxurious warmth to the guest rooms. *Singel 303–309 (near Spui).* ☎ *020/ 624-5146. www.estherea.nl. 95 units. Doubles 190€–285€. Free WiFi. Tram: 1, 2, or 5 to Spui. Map p 124.*

★★ **Hampshire Amsterdam American Hotel** LEIDSEPLEIN Built in 1900, this hotel boasts Venetian Gothic and Art Nouveau architectural features, while guest rooms are modern. Rooms are subdued, refined, and superbly furnished. Some have views of the Singelgracht canal, while others overlook kaleidoscopic Leidseplein. *Leidsekade 97 (at Leidseplein).* ☎ *020/556-3000. www.hampshire-hotels.com. 175 units. Doubles 144€– 311€. Free WiFi. Tram: 1, 2, or 5 to Leidseplein. Map p 124.*

★ **Hampshire Hotel Lancaster Amsterdam** OOST A stone's throw from Artis Zoo and a short walk from the Tropenmuseum and the Botanical Gardens, this hotel is in a great location for families. The quiet neighborhood seems far from the hustle and bustle of the old center, but is just a 10-minute tram ride away. Attractive triple rooms are perfect if you're traveling with kids. *Plantage Middenlaan 48 (at Plantage Westermanlaan).* ☎ *020/ 535-6888. www.hampshire-hotels. com. 91 units. Doubles 138€–188€ w/ breakfast. Free WiFi. Tram: 9 or 14 to Plantage Kerklaan. Map p 124.*

★ **Hilton Amsterdam** NIEUW ZUID The infamous room no. 902 is where John Lennon and Yoko Ono had their "Bed-in for Peace" in 1969. Designers consulted Yoko when renovating the room, and it now features extensive use of natural materials. The hotel has modern facilities and a location in a leafy, almost suburban district. *Apollolaan 138 (at Breitnerstraat).* ☎ *020/710-6000. www.placeshilton.com/ amsterdam. 271 units. Doubles 249€–369€. Free WiFi. Tram: 5 or 24 to Apollolaan. Map p 123.*

★ **Hoksbergen** CANAL RING This attractive budget hotel is housed in a 300-year-old canal house and offers small but bright and clean rooms at affordable rates. Rooms at the front have canal views. There's no elevator, but there are five newly appointed apartments nearby that are perfect for families. *Singel 301 (near Spui).* ☎ *020/626-6043. www.hotel hoksbergen.com. 19 units. Doubles 70€–135€ w/breakfast. Free WiFi. Tram: 1, 2, or 5 to Spui. Map p 124.*

★★ **Hotel de l'Europe** OLD CENTER This classic luxury hotel commands a prime riverside location. The rooms are plush, spacious, and bright, and all boast marble bathrooms. There's a stellar restaurant (Bord'Eau), a spa, and a summer terrace overlooking the Amstel. *Nieuwe Doelenstraat 2–14 (facing Muntplein).* ☎ *020/531-1777. www.leurope.nl. 111 units. Doubles 450€–720€. Free WiFi. Tram: 4, 9, 14, 16, or 24 to Muntplein. Map p 124.*

★ **Keizershof** CANAL RING This four-story canal house dates to 1672. A grand piano in the hotel's lounge adds a certain stateliness to the place. Rooms are beamed and cozy with simple, modern furnishings, but only two have private bathrooms; others have showers in the room but shared WC. In summer, you can enjoy your huge breakfast in the flower-filled courtyard. There's no elevator. *Keizersgracht 618 (at Nieuwe Spiegelstraat).* ☎ *020/622-2855. www.hotel keizershof.nl. 6 units. Doubles 95€– 130€ w/breakfast. Tram: 7, 10, 16, or 24 to Keizersgracht. Map p 125.*

★★ **Lloyd Hotel & Cultural Embassy** WATERFRONT This historic Amsterdam School–style hotel in the up-and-coming Eastern Docklands boasts a wide variety of accommodations, from tiny rooms to impressive suites and duplexes; one even has a grand piano and a sweeping staircase. Most are kitted

Hotel de l'Europe.

A stylish bathroom at the Lloyd Hotel.

out by contemporary Dutch architects and designers; there are frequent exhibitions and shows here, too. *Oostelijke Handelskade 34 (at IJhaven).* ☎ *020/561-3636. www.lloydhotel.com. 117 units. Doubles 85€–500€. Free WiFi. Tram: 10 or 26 to Rietlandpark. Map p 125.*

★★★ Mauro Mansion OLD

CENTER Currently riding high on the Amsterdam list of hot hotels, Mauro Mansion is the antithesis of a bland chain hotel. This little gem is a nine-room treasure trove of quirky design hidden in a 16th-century canal house overlooking Geldersekade. Several bedrooms have views over the canal and all are a stylish clash of old and new—wardrobes made of industrial piping, hammocks, beds swathed in net, shiny rubber flooring, and pristine white-tiled bathrooms. No children under 12. *Geldersekade 16 (off Prins Hendrikkade).* ☎ *061/297-4594. www.mauromansion.com. 9 units. Doubles 120€–1,200€. Free WiFi. Walk from Centraal Station. Map p 125.*

★ Mercure Amsterdam Arthur

Frommer CANAL RING This stylish, friendly hotel once owned by Arthur Frommer is tucked away on a side street behind Prinsengracht. Converted from weavers' cottages, the rooms are not huge but are stylish, with soft pastel colors. There's a cozy bar. *Noorderstraat 46 (off Vijzelgracht).* ☎ *020/721-9175. www.mercure.com. 93 units. Doubles 159€–209€ w/breakfast. Free WiFi. Tram: 16 or 24 to Prinsengracht. Map p 125.*

★ NH Grand Hotel Krasnapol-

sky OLD CENTER Smack in the midst of it all, the "Kras" faces the Royal Palace (see p 12) and is an Amsterdam landmark. The sizes and shapes of the rooms vary considerably, and the upkeep on them is variable. Although the renovations have finished, there have

A cozy but minimalist loft room at Mauro Mansion.

A Canal-House Warning

Elevators are difficult things to shoehorn into the cramped confines of a 17th-century canal house and cost more than some moderately priced and budget hotels can afford. Consequently, many simply don't have them. If lugging your old wooden sea chest up six flights of steep, narrow stairs is liable to void your life insurance, better make sure an elevator is in place and working. Should there be no such amenity, you might want to ask for a room on a lower floor.

recently been some quibbles about service. *Dam 9.* ☎ *020/554-9111. www.nh-hotels.com. 468 units. Doubles 179€–374€. Free WiFi in lobby. Tram: 1, 2, 4, 5, 9, 13, 14, 16, 17, or 24 to the Dam. Map p 125.*

★★ **Owl** MUSEUM DISTRICT
This solid bargain choice is just a few minutes' walk from Leidseplein, but in a quiet spot. Rooms are fairly compact, with oak furnishings and whitewashed walls. There's a bar and a small garden, great for lounging on a warm summer day. *Roemer Visscherstraat 1 (off Stadhouderskade).* ☎ *020/618-9484. www.owl-hotel.nl. 34 units. Doubles 120€–158€ w/breakfast. Free WiFi. Tram: 3 or 10 to Van Baerlestraat. Map p 123.*

★ **Piet Hein** MUSEUM DISTRICT
Set in an Art Nouveau villa, this boutique hotel is decorated in tones of gray and black. A cool, contemporary style permeates the public spaces and most of the guest rooms. Unwind in the evenings in the relaxed bar/lounge or out on the garden terrace. *Vossiusstraat 52–53 (facing Vondelpark).* ☎ *020/662-7205. www.hotelpiet hein.com. 81 units. Doubles 79€–235€ w/breakfast. Free WiFi. Tram: 2 or 5 to Van Gogh Museum. Map p 123.*

★ **Prinsenhof** CANAL RING This canal-house hotel offers basic but

comfortable rooms with beamed ceilings; not all have bathrooms. Front rooms look out onto the Prinsengracht, where colorful houseboats are moored. There's no elevator, but a pulley hauls your luggage up and down the stairs. *Prinsengracht 810 (at Utrechtsestraat).* ☎ *020/623-1772. www. hotelprinsenhof.com. 11 units. Doubles 60€–100€ w/breakfast. Free WiFi. Tram: 4 to Prinsengracht. Map p 125.*

★★★ **Pulitzer** CANAL RING
The award-winning Pulitzer offers its lucky guests pure luxury without being ostentatious. A superior location on a canal at the edge of the Jordaan, rooms so plush you sink into them, a spa, a fantastic restaurant, and a wine bar make this a good place to splurge on a romantic getaway. It's also close to the tourist hotspots and the pretty streets of Jordaan. *Prinsengracht 315–331 (at Westermarkt).* ☎ *020/ 523-5235. www.pulitzeramsterdam. com. 230 units. Doubles 309€–706€. Tram: 13, 14, or 17 to Westermarkt. Map p 125.*

★ **Radisson Blu** OLD CENTER
This sprawling hotel is close to everything. There are four room categories, so be sure to state your preference when you reserve; the superior rooms have recently been

Many rooms at the Pulitzer overlook a charming canal.

spruced up. The Dutch rooms come with oak furnishings and orange curtains; the Scandinavian, Asian, and Art Deco rooms are sparser and airier. The hotel has a gym, a full restaurant, and the Pastorie Bar serving snacky meals. *Rusland 17 (at the University of Amsterdam).* ☎ *020/623-1231. www.radissonblu. com. 252 units. Doubles 190€–260€ w/breakfast (but not standard rooms). Free WiFi. Tram: 4, 9, 14, 16, or 24 to Spui. Map p 125.*

★★ **Renaissance Amsterdam**
OLD CENTER The Renaissance is a standout among the city's large

business hotels, tucked away off a charming canal just a 5-minute walk from Centraal Station. It feels much cozier than you'd expect from its size. Rooms are very spacious, with picture windows and large bathrooms. The staff are extremely helpful and courteous. *Kattengat 1 (at Singel).* ☎ *020/621-2223. www. renaissanceamsterdam.nl. 402 units. Doubles 219€–399€. Tram: 1, 2, 5, 13, or 17 to Martelaarsgracht. Map p 125.*

★★ **Sandton Hotel De Filosoof**
MUSEUM DISTRICT You'll find this small, friendly hotel in a quiet,

Money-Saving Tips

The Netherlands adheres to the Benelux Hotel Classification system, which awards stars to hotels based on set criteria—having a pool, an elevator, and so forth. Each establishment must display a sign indicating its classification, from "1" for those with minimum amenities to "5" for deluxe, full-service hotels. Amsterdam's hotels can be expensive. If a particular hotel strikes your fancy but is out of your price range, it may pay to inquire if special off-season, weekend, specific weekday, or other packages will bring prices down to what you can afford; with many hotels, it's cheaper to book with them directly online rather than going through an agency. Some hotels will offer significant rate reductions between November 1 and March 31 to fill the rooms, except during the Christmas and New Year period.

leafy and upscale residential neighborhood not far from the **Vondelpark** (see p 15). Rooms are small but charming, and some are very bright, with large wood-framed windows. They're individually decorated in themes that reflect various philosophies; choose from the Golden Age–style Spinoza room, or the simply decorated Thoreau room. *Anna van den Vondelstraat 6 (off Overtoom).* ☎ *020/683-3013. www.sandton.eu. 38 units. Doubles 109€–194€. Free WiFi. Tram: 1 to Jan Pieter Heijestraat. Map p 123.*

★★★ **Seven Bridges** CANAL RING   This canal-house gem is quite simply gorgeous. Each individually decorated room boasts antique furnishings (Art Deco, Biedermeier, Louis XVI, rococo), handmade Italian drapes, and wood-tiled floors. Attic rooms have sloped ceilings and exposed wood beams. It's the perfect romantic hideaway, and very reasonable in price considering its style and opulence. *Reguliersgracht 31 (at Keizersgracht).* ☎ *020/623-1329. www.sevenbridges hotel.nl. 11 units. Doubles 95€–205€. Free WiFi. Tram: 16 or 24 to Keizersgracht. Map p 125.*

★★ **Seven One Seven** CANAL RING   Hardly a budget option, this suite-only and award-winning palace of style is wonderfully furnished in lavish 19th-century style, with every possible amenity on tap. An elegant drawing room, a sunspot terrace, views over the canal, a flower-filled breakfast room, and smooth service all contribute to making this a truly unforgettable experience in Amsterdam, far removed from impersonal chain hotels. A little irritant is the extra charge for breakfast over and above an already expensive stay. *Prinsengracht 717 (at Leidseplein).* ☎ *020/427-0717. 717hotel.nl. 9 units. Doubles 275€–450€. Free WiFi. Tram: 1, 2, or 5 to Prinsengracht. Map p 125.*

★★ **Winston** OLD CENTER   Young partygoers flock to this vibrant budget-cum-art hotel with two bars and a rowdy nightclub on the premises. It's on a somewhat seedy street, mere steps from the Red Light District. The hotel motto is "party hard, sleep easy." That says it all, really. Families may want to look elsewhere, but it's a great choice for young party people. *Warmoesstraat 129 (off Damrak).* ☎ *020/623-1380. www.winston.nl. 69 units. Doubles 89€–130€ w/breakfast. Tram: 1, 2, 4, 5, 9, 13, 14, 16, 17, or 24 to the Dam. Map p 125.* ●

Summer Stays: Reserve Ahead

Despite there being nearly 400 hotels in the city, May through September are tough months for finding hotel rooms in Amsterdam. Try to reserve as far ahead as possible for this period. If you have problems getting a room, sit it out on the web or contact the tourist information agency I amsterdam, which will generally be able to help.

You can reserve hotel rooms through (among other organizations) the **I amsterdam visitor information centers** at Stationsplein 10 and Schiphol Plaza at the airport (☎ **020/702-6000;** www.iamsterdam.com).

10 The Best Day Trips & Excursions

Haarlem

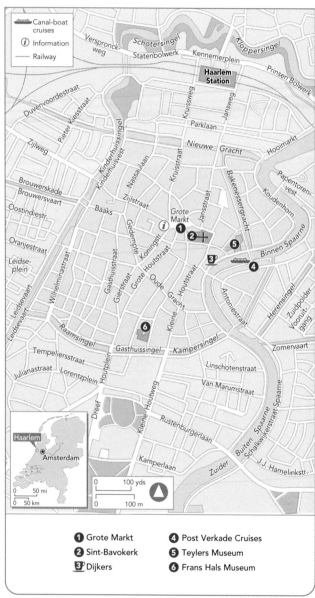

Canal-boat cruises
(i) Information
Railway

1 Grote Markt

2 Sint-Bavokerk

3 Dijkers

4 Post Verkade Cruises

5 Teylers Museum

6 Frans Hals Museum

Previous page: Haarlem's Sint-Bavokerk (St. Bavo's Church).

Handsome Haarlem is today virtually a suburb of Amsterdam, but in the Dutch Golden Age it was a thriving town and cultural center, home of Rembrandt's contemporaries Frans Hals, Jacob van Ruisdael, and Pieter Saenredam, who were famous for their detailed portraits, landscapes, and church interiors. Despite its diminutive size, a day in Haarlem reveals one of the finest churches in The Netherlands, a charismatic muddle of architecture, and one of the best art galleries in Europe. START: **A walk of 800m (½ mile) south from the station along Kruisweg, Kruisstraat, and Smedestraat to Grote Markt.**

Grote Markt.

❶ ★★★ **Grote Markt.** The monumental buildings around this tree-lined square, which date from the 15th to 19th centuries, are a delightful visual minicourse in the development of Dutch architecture. The oldest building is the 14th-century gabled, balconied, and spired Stadhuis (Town Hall), a former hunting lodge that was rebuilt in the 17th century. ○ *30 min. Market Mon 8:30am–5pm; Sat 9am–5pm.*

❷ ★ **Sint-Bavokerk (St. Bavo's Church).** Completed in 1520, this magnificent Gothic church—also known as the Grote Kerk (Great Church)—dominates the Grote

Markt and has a rare unity of structure and proportion. Its elegant wooden tower is adorned with gilt and topped with a gilded crown.

St. Bavo's famed Christian Müller organ.

Explore Haarlem's canals with a boat ride on Post Verkade Cruises.

The light and airy church interior has whitewashed walls and sandstone pillars, but the standout feature is the famous, soaring Christian Müller organ (1738), which has 5,068 pipes and is nearly 30m (98 ft.) tall. Mozart played the organ in 1766 when he was just 10 years old, and Handel and Liszt both made pilgrimages to play here. You can hear the organ in free recitals from May to October, at occasional Saturday performances by the church organists (tickets 3€), and also in a program of services, festivals, and concerts running throughout the summer; check the website for details. ① *45 min. Grote Markt 22.* ☎ *023/553-2040. www.bavo.nl. Admission 2.50€ adults, 1€ kids 12–16. Mar 24–Sept Mon–Sat 10am–5pm; Oct–Mar 23 Mon–Sat 10am–4pm.*

③ ★ Dijkers. This tiny, stylish restaurant offers light lunches from a menu of BLTs, salads, *bitterballen,* and nachos for a lunchtime pit stop. *Warmoesstraat 5–7.* ☎ *023/551-1564. www.restaurant dijkers.nl. $.*

Haarlem Basics

Haarlem is so easily accessible from Amsterdam that many people commute daily; this charming town is a mere 15 minutes from Amsterdam Centraal Station, and trains run between the two at regular intervals. The round-trip fare is 8€. Once in Haarlem, it's easy to get around on foot; the station is a 10-minute walk from Grote Markt.

The **VVV Haarlem** (tourist office) is at Grote Markt 2 (☎ **023/531-7325;** www.haarlemmarketing.nl). Opening hours are April through September Monday to Friday from 9:30am to 5:30pm, Saturday from 10am to 5pm, and Sunday from noon to 4pm; October through March Monday from 1 to 5:30pm, Tuesday to Friday from 9:30am to 5:30pm, and Saturday from 10am to 5pm.

④ ★★ Post Verkade Cruises.

A canal cruise is the ideal way to explore Haarlem if you're time-deprived. The dock is on the River Spaarne just beside the Gravenstenenbrug, a handsome lift bridge. You'll see loads of historical buildings and pass close to an 18th-century traditional Dutch windmill—a great photo op. ⏱ *50 min. Spaarne 11a on the riverside. tel] 023/535-7723. www.postverkadegroep.nl. Tickets 11€ adults, 5.50€ kids 2–8. Boats depart daily at noon, 1, 2, 3, and 4pm.*

⑤ ★★ kids Teylers Museum.

Quirky but oddly compelling, this museum was the very first to open in The Netherlands, in 1784. It's named after the 18th-century merchant Pieter Teyler van der Hulst, who willed his entire fortune to the

Kids will love the odd inventions on display at the Teylers Museum.

Gisteren typte ze nog . . .

Vanaf vandaag automatiseert zij feilloos uw gehele korrespondentie

advancement of art and science. You'll find a diverse collection here: drawings by Michelangelo, Raphael, and Rembrandt (which are shown in rotation); fossils, minerals, and skeletons; instruments of physics; and an odd assortment of inventions, including the largest electrostatic generator in the world. ⏱ *1½ hr. Spaarne 16.* ☎ *023/531-9010. www.teylersmuseum.eu. 11€ adults, 2€ kids 6–18. Tues–Sat 10am–5pm; Sun and holidays noon–5pm. Closed Jan 1, Dec 25.*

⑥ ★★★ Frans Hals Museum.

Quite simply the highlight of many art lovers' trips to Holland, this museum is housed in an elegant former almshouse (see p 50) dating from 1608 during the Dutch Golden Age. Consequently, the wonderful paintings by Frans Hals (1580–1686) and other masters of the Haarlem School hang in a setting reminiscent of the 17th-century houses they were intended to adorn. A dynamic new exhibition, "The Hals Phenomenon," provides an informative introduction to this great artist, who earned a living by painting portraits of members of the local guilds (see p 168). Five of his civic-guard pictures are on display in the museum, including *A Banquet of the Officers of the Civic Guard of St George* (1616), alongside individual portraits and generic Dutch scenes. Among other highlights of the collections are a superb dollhouse from around 1750 and fine collections of antiques, silver, porcelain, and clocks. ⏱ *2 hr. Groot Heiligland 62.* ☎ *023/511-5775. www.franshalsmuseum.com. Admission 12.50€ adults, 6€ students 19–24, free for kids 18 and under. Tues–Sat 11am–5pm; Sun noon–5pm. Closed Jan 1, Apr 27, and Dec 25.*

Delft

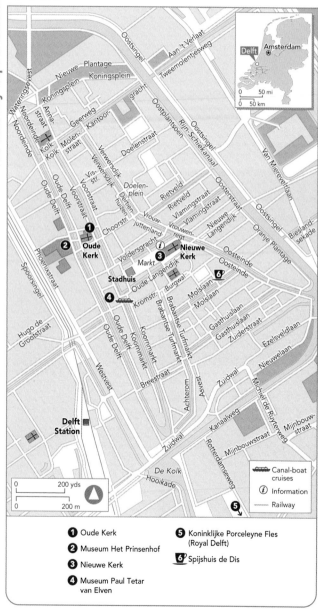

Amsterdam
Delft

0   50 mi
0   50 km

Canal-boat cruises

(i) Information

Railway

0   200 yds
0   200 m

❶ Oude Kerk

❷ Museum Het Prinsenhof

❸ Nieuwe Kerk

❹ Museum Paul Tetar van Elven

❺ Koninklijke Porceleyne Fles (Royal Delft)

6' Spijshuis de Dis

Delft is best known as the home of the famous blue-and-white porcelain. On this day out, you'll visit the factory where it's produced. Delft is a small, charming city with a big history; it was the cradle of the Dutch Republic, the burial place of the royal family, and the birthplace and inspiration of artist Jan Vermeer, the 17th-century master of light and subtle emotion. Take a stroll through the streets to admire the colorful flower boxes and linden trees bending over tranquil canals. START: **Walk north from the station along canalside Oude Delft and through the heart of the Old Town, a distance of around 800m (½ mile).**

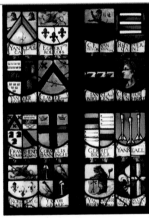

A stained-glass window from Delft's Oude Kerk.

❶ ★★ Oude Kerk (Old Church).

Jan Vermeer's house is long gone, as are his paintings, but he's buried at the Oude Kerk, an immense church with 13th-century origins that has been much added to through the years. The Gothic north transept was appended in the 16th century, and the ornate, skinny clock tower was rebuilt after the local arsenal blew up and destroyed much of the town in 1654; the repairs have left it with a distinct kink in its profile. Like many Dutch churches, the floors are paved with tomb slabs from the 17th century, and dappled with sunlight streaming through the glorious stained-glass windows, which are the work of 20th-century craftsman Joep Nicolas. ⏱ *30 min. Heilige Geestkerkhof 25.* ☎ *015/212-3015. oudeennieuwe kerkdelft.nl. Admission (combined with Nieuwe Kerk; see below) 3.50€ adults, 2€ students 12–25, 1.50€ kids 6–11. Mon–Sat 10am–5pm.*

A statue of William I of Orange outside the Museum Het Prinsenhof.

Delft Basics

Delft is just under an hour by train from Amsterdam. The round-trip fare is 25€, and trains depart Centraal Station every 30 minutes. From Delft station, almost everything is just a 10-minute walk. The tourist office is the **Touristen Informatie Punt (TIP)** at Kerkstraat 3 (☎ 015/215-4051; www.delft.nl), in the center of town near the Nieuwe Kerk. Opening hours are April to September, Monday and Saturday from 10am to 5pm, Tuesday to Friday from 9am to 6pm, Sunday from 10am to 4pm; October to March, Tuesday to Saturday from 10am to 4pm, Sunday from 11am to 3pm.

❷ ★★ **Museum Het Prinsenhof.** The "Father of the Dutch Nation," William I of Orange had his headquarters in this Gothic former convent during the years he

Delft's Nieuwe Kerk.

was fighting the Spanish to found the Dutch Republic. He was assassinated here in 1584, and you can still see the musket-ball holes in the stairwell. Today the Prinsenhof relates the story of William's life and displays paintings, tapestries, silverware, and pottery from the 17th century. Don't miss the cleverly lit and detailed features of every militiaman's face in Michiel Jansz van Mierevelt's *Civic Guard Banquet* (1611) on the top floor. There is also a beautiful collection of Golden Age glassware. ◷ 1 hr. *Sint-Agathaplein 1.* ☎ *015/260-2358. www.prinsenhof-delft.nl. Admission 8.50€ adults, 5€ students and kids 12–18. Tues–Sun 11am–5pm. Closed Jan 1, Easter Mon, Apr 27, Pentecost Mon, and Dec 25.*

❸ ★ **Nieuwe Kerk.** Prince William of Orange and other members of the House of Oranje-Nassau are buried in this church, built between 1383 and 1510. Like many of Delft's medieval buildings, it was restored following a fire in 1536. Architect and sculptor Hendrick de Keyser designed the ornate black-and-white marble tomb of William of Orange in 1621. Renowned architect Pierre Cuypers, designer of the **Rijksmuseum** in Amsterdam (see

You can see artists at work at Delft's porcelain factory.

p 7), added the 100m (328 ft.) tower to the Gothic facade in 1872. After exploring the interior, climb the landmark spire for glorious views over Delft. ⓘ *30 min. Markt 80.* ☎ *015/212-3015. oudeennieuwe kerkdelft.nl. Admission: Church (combined with Oude Kerk; see above) 3.50€ adults, 2€ students 12–25, 1.50€ kids 6–11; Tower: 3.50€ adults, 2€ students 12–25, 1.50€ kids 6–11. Mon–Sat 10am–7pm.*

❹ ★★ Museum Paul Tetar van Elven. The 19th-century artist Van Elven (1823–96) lived and worked in this stately canal house, and the furnishings are just as he left them. His 17th-century-style studio looks like it's ready for the artist to enter and pick up his brushes. Van Elven's furniture and porcelain form one of the finest collections of 19th-century decorative arts in a beautifully restored interior, but more interesting are the paintings. Van Elven was a noted copyist, and many of his reproductions are on display. Except for a subpar Vermeer on the

second floor, most of his fakes are excellent, especially the Rembrandts and the Paulus Potter on the first floor. ⓘ *45 min. Koornmarkt 67 (south of Markt).* ☎ *015/ 212-4206. www.museumpaultetar vanelven.nl. Admission 5€ adults, 2.50€ kids 12–18. Tues–Sun 1–5pm.*

❺ ★ Koninklijke Porceleyne Fles (Royal Delft). If you like Delftware porcelain, you'll be in heaven at the Royal Delft. The experience includes a visit to the factory and a firsthand view of the business of painting porcelain; a visit to the Delft museum, which features antique multi-spouted tulip vases; and the obligatory showroom for factory seconds at relative bargain prices. The highlights of any visit are the workshops where you can paint your own porcelain, which is fired, glazed, and ready for pickup (or shipping overseas) in 48 hours. The price quoted for the workshops includes materials but not shipping; workshops must be reserved at least 24 hours in advance. ⓘ *2 hr. Rotterdamseweg 196.* ☎ *015/251-2030. www.royal delft.com. Tour 12€ adults, free for kids 11 and under; workshops 38€– 40€. Mar 17–Oct 31 daily 9am–5pm; Nov–Mar 16 Mon–Sat 9am–5pm, Sun noon–5pm. Closed Jan 1 and Dec 25–26.*

❻ ★★ Spijshuis de Dis. Great Dutch cooking is dished up at this atmospheric restaurant. Traditional plates are presented in modern variations: *bokkenpot* (a stew made from beef, chicken, and rabbit in beer sauce), lamb served with rosemary, and a delicious fresh fish and seafood platter for sharing. *Beestenmarkt 36.* ☎ *015/213-1782. www. spijshuisdedis.com. Tues–Sat 5–10pm. $$.*

Rotterdam

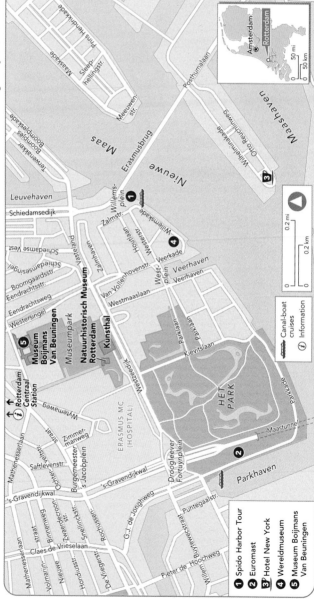

1 Spido Harbor Tour
2 Euromast
3 Hotel New York
4 Wereldmuseum
5 Museum Bojimans Van Beuningen

Canal-boat cruises
i Information

Bisected by the Maas, Rotterdam was virtually flattened by Nazi bombing during World War II but has sprung phoenix-like back to life with a vengeance. It is a city looking forward, full of innovative architecture along the river that brings in its wealth. The city also plays an important part in American history: Delfshaven, one of the few historic districts still intact, is the port from which the Pilgrim Fathers sailed to the New World. START: **Metro train to Leuvehaven, or tram to the Spido tour-boat dock on the Maas.**

Explore Rotterdam's busy port from a Spido Harbor Tours cruise.

❶ ★★★ kids **Spido Harbor Tours.** Take one of Spido's boat tours up and down the River Maas to discover the workings of one of the world's largest ports and its fine modern architecture. You travel under the city's iconic landmark Erasmus Bridge (or Swan Bridge, as it's known by the locals); pass historic Delfshaven, the departure point for the Pilgrim Fathers as they left for Massachusetts in the U.S. in 1620; and get fabulous views of the Euromast, Rotterdam's tallest structure. But the most fascinating aspect of this tour is its up-close-and-personal view of the workings of this immense port as the boat zigzags around giant cranes, tankers, barges, and all sizes of boats and ships. Older kids and anybody with a maritime interest will love this trip. ⓘ *75 min. Willemsplein 85 (under the Erasmus Bridge).* ☎ *010/275-9988. spido.nl. Tickets 11€ adults, 7€ kids 4–11. Apr–Sept departures every 45 min from 10am; Oct–Mar usually 4 trips per day, the last one at 3:30pm; check website for winter hours. Tram: 7 to Willemsplein.*

❷ ★★ **Euromast.** This slender tower, 185m (607 ft.) tall, is indisputably the best vantage point for an overall view of Rotterdam and its environs, out to 30km (19 miles) on a clear day. You can have lunch or dinner in the Euromast Brasserie, 96m (314 ft.) above the harbor park, while enjoying spectacular views of the port. A rotating elevator departs from here for the

Rotterdam Basics

Up to 10 trains per hour depart from Amsterdam's Centraal Station for Rotterdam Centraal Station. On NS Hispeed trains, the ride takes 40 minutes, and on InterCity trains the journey is 70 minutes. The round-trip fare is 29€. Once in Rotterdam, you can use the trams and the Metro with the same OV-chipkaart public transportation card used in Amsterdam (see p 160). Taxis are plentiful, too.

A tourist information center at the railway station, **VVV Rotterdam Centraal,** Stationsplein 45 (no phone; www.rotterdam. info), is open daily from 9am to 5:30pm. A second tourist office is **ROTTERDAM.INFO** on Binnenwegplein at Coolsingel 195–197 (☎ **010/790-0185;** www.rotterdam.info; Metro: Beurs). This office is open daily from 9:30am to 6pm.

Euroscoop viewing platform at the top of the spire. From the Brasserie level, for an additional fee (53€), you can abseil or rope-slide back to the ground—definitely not for the faint of heart. ⏱ *30 min. Parkhaven (by Spido's mooring).* ☎ *010/436-4811. www.euromast.nl. Admission 9€ adults, 6€ kids 4–11. Apr–Sept daily 9:30am–11pm; Oct–Mar daily 10am–11pm. Tram: 8 to Euromast.*

3 ★★ **Hotel New York.** The former HQ of the Holland-America Line, which carried hundreds of thousands of Europeans to a new life in the U.S., is now a hotel with a smart restaurant overlooking the river. It's at Wilhelmina Pier on the south side of the Maas in Kop van Zuid, 5 minutes by water taxi from Euromast (☎ 010/403-0303; www. watertaxirotterdam.nl). Settle at a table and enjoy afternoon tea with cake and scones, or splash out in the waterside oyster bar. *Koninginnenhoofd 1.* ☎ *010/439-0500. www. hotelnewyork.nl. $$.*

4 ★★ **Wereldmuseum.** Reflecting the rich maritime heritage of The Netherlands, the World Art Museum has squirreled together thousands of historic artifacts from across the world, many picked up by Dutch sailors during the 17th-century Golden Age. The result is beautiful, vibrant, and unusual displays of tribal artwork not seen anywhere else, from Tibetan prayer flags to primitive Australian Aboriginal paintings and beautiful Indonesian hand-printed batiks, showcased along with African carvings and a luscious collection of silk textiles embroidered in gold. The museum is in a lovely white Art Nouveau building; its classy restaurant has views out across Rotterdam harbor. ⏱ *90 min. Willemskade 22–25.* ☎ *010/270-7172. www. wereldmuseum.nl. Admission 12.50€ adults, free for kids 12 and under. Tues–Sun 10:30am–5:30pm. Closed Jan 1, Apr 27, and Dec 25. Tram: 5 to Westerplein.*

5 ★★★ **Museum Boijmans Van Beuningen.** Another great Dutch treasure trove of fine art is in Rotterdam's foremost museum.

Visitors with a Magritte at the Museum Boijmans Van Beuningen.

Housed in a redbrick, modernist-style gallery with airy glass extensions are exhibits that run from paintings from Old Dutch Masters to contemporary glassware to a fine ensemble of porcelain, silver, and Delftware. Highlights of the 140,000-strong works of art include Pieter Bruegel's peerless *The Tower of Babel* (c. 1553) and Rembrandt's sensitive *Titus at His Desk* (1655), a masterly play on light and shadow. Other great names in this carefully curated museum include Dalí, Da Vinci, Monet, Picasso, Van Eyck, Man Ray, and the funky furniture of Gerrit Rietveld. There's a landscaped sculpture park to explore outside and lots of heavyweight temporary exhibitions. ⏱ *2 hr. Museumpark 18–20.* ☎ *010/441-9400 (weekends* ☎ *010/441-9475). www.boijmans.nl. Admission 13€ adults, 10€ seniors, 6€ students, free for kids 17 and under. Tues–Sun 11am–5pm. Closed Jan 1, Apr 27, and Dec 25. Tram: 7 or 20 to Museumpark.*

A Grand Harbor

A dredged deepwater channel connects Rotterdam with the North Sea and forms a 40km-long (25-mile) harbor. The Port of Rotterdam is the world's third-busiest port after Shanghai and Singapore and is the pump that feeds Europe's commercial arteries. The port authority handles around 35,000 ships and 450 million metric tons of cargo annually. A trip around the harbor may be one of the more unusual experiences to be had in The Netherlands, but the sheer scale of the operation will make your jaw drop. Container ships, cargo

A view of the port city of Rotterdam.

carriers, tankers, and careworn tramps are waited on, 24 hours a day, by a vast retinue of people and machines; trucks, trains, and barges all rush back and forth in a blur of activity.

The Hague & Scheveningen

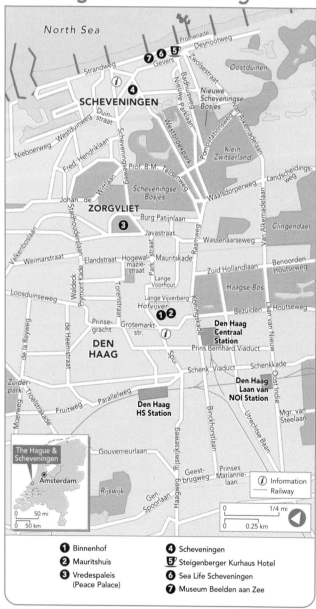

North Sea

Promenade

Deynootweg

Strandweg

⑦ ⑥ ⑤

Gevers

Zwolsestraat

Oostduinen

ⓘ

④

SCHEVENINGEN

Duin-

straat

Nieuwe

Scheveningse

Bosjes

Nieboerweg

Westduinweg

Fred. Hendriklaan

Wittlaan

Scheveningseweg

Nieuwe Parklaan

Badhuisweg

Westbroekpark

Pompstationsweg

van Alkemadelaan

Klein

Zwitserland

Prof. B.M. Teldenweg

Johan de Wittlaan

ZORGVLIET

Scheveningse

Bosjes

Waalsdorperweg

Landscheidings-

weg

Stadhouderslaan

Burg Patijnlaan

Valkenboslaan

③

Javastraat

Wassenaarseweg

Clingendael

Weimarstraat

Elandstraat

Hogewal

mazie-

straat

Mauritskade

Parkstraat

Rapenweg

Zuid Hollandlaan

Benoorden

Houtseweg

Loosduinseweg

Waldeck

Pymont Kade

Torenstraat

Lange

Voorhout

Lange Vijverberg

Haagse Bos

Van Alkemadelaan

de la Reyweg

de Heemstraat

Prinse-

gracht

Hofvijver

① ②

ⓘ

Koningskade

Bezuiden

Laan van Nieuw

Oost Indie

DEN

HAAG

Grotemarkt-

str.

Den Haag

Centraal

Station

Spui

Prins Bernhard Viaduct

Zuider-

park

Toelstrakade

Moerweg

Parallelweg

Schenk Viaduct

Schenkkade

Den Haag

Laan van

NOI Station

Fruitweg

Den Haag

HS Station

Binckhorstlaan

Utrechtse Baan

Mgr. van

Steelaan

Gouverneurlaan

Rijswijkseweg

Geest-

brugweg

Prinses

Marianne-

laan

ⓘ Information

— Railway

Rijswijk

Haagweg

Gen.

Spoorlaan

The Hague &

Scheveningen

★

Amsterdam

0 ___ 50 mi

0 ___ 50 km

0 ___ 1/4 mi

0 ___ 0.25 km

① Binnenhof

② Mauritshuis

③ Vredespaleis

(Peace Palace)

④ Scheveningen

⑤ Steigenberger Kurhaus Hotel

⑥ Sea Life Scheveningen

⑦ Museum Beelden aan Zee

The stately and grand capital of The Netherlands contrasts with its laidback seacoast neighbor Scheveningen, where you'll get a bracing taste of escapist beach life. Visiting The Hague (Den Haag in Dutch) gives a glimpse into Dutch political life with a tour of the Binnenhof, the historic seat of Dutch Parliament, and a chance to visit the Peace Palace, home to the International Court of Justice, as well as access to the sublime art collection at the newly refurbished Mauritshuis. START: **A 10-minute tram ride from Centraal Station to Buitenhof, the Outer Court of the Dutch Parliament.**

Binnenhof courtyard.

❶ ★★ Binnenhof (Inner Court).

A venerable complex of historic civic buildings, the Binnenhof is the home of Dutch Parliament. The many-gabled, medieval Ridderzaal (Hall of the Knights) is the most striking building, built in 1280, with a vast, vaulted interior. The hall plays a leading part in Dutch politics; King Willem-Alexander delivers his annual Speech from the Throne from here on Prinsjesdag (third Tues in Sept). The Binnenhof is grouped around courtyards that are free to wander, but if you want to see inside the Ridderzaal, the Dutch House of Representatives, or the Senate, you have to join a guided tour. What you get to see depends on what's happening in Parliament that day. ⏱ *90 min. Binnenhof 8A.* ☎ *070/757-0200. www.prodemos.nl. Tickets 5€–8.50€, depending on tour. Guided tours start from the Binnenhof Visitor Centre at Hofweg 1. Call ahead or book online; tours and start times vary. Tram: 1, 2, 3, 6, 7, 8, 9, 16, or 17 to Buitenhof.*

❷ ★★★ Mauritshuis.

Situated on Hofvijver Lake to the right of the Binnenhof, the Mauritshuis is scheduled to reopen in June 2014 to reveal new galleries and exhibition spaces as well as a careful facelift to this fine 17th-century townhouse. Its astounding, heavy-weight collection of Dutch Old Master showpieces has been traveling the world but will return for the

The Best Day Trips & Excursions

Vermeer's famous Girl with a Pearl Earring at the Mauritshuis.

gallery opening. You'll see fabulous works of art, including *View of Delft* and *Girl with a Pearl Earring* by Jan Vermeer, Carel Fabritius' adorable *Goldfinch*, and the famous Holbein portrait of Jane Seymour, third wife of England's much-married King Henry VIII. ⏱ *2 hr. Korte Vijververg 8.* ☎ *070/302-3435. www.maurits huis.nl. Call or check the website for admission and opening hours. Tram: 1, 2, 3, 6, 7, 8, 9, 16, or 17 to Buitenhof.*

❸ ★★ **Vredespaleis (Peace Palace).** U.S. philanthropist Andrew Carnegie donated over a million dollars to the construction of this magnificent mock-Gothic palace, home to the International Court of Justice and the Permanent Court of Arbitration. The building was designed by French architect Louis Cordonnier and completed in 1913; today it can be visited only by guided tour. You'll be able to visit most of the ornate apartments and marvel at gifts given by each of the participating countries: crystal chandeliers (each weighing 1,750kg/3,858 lb.) from Delft, made with real rubies and emeralds; incredible mosaic floors from France; a huge Turkish carpet woven in 1926 in Izmir; and an immense 3,500kg (7,716 lb.) vase from Czar Nicholas of Russia. If the courts are not in session, your guide will take you inside the International Court of Justice, which handles all of the United Nations' judicial cases. The new visitor center highlights the history of the Peace Palace with an exhibition and short film. ⏱ *90 min. Carnegieplein 2.* ☎ *070/302-4242. www.vredes paleis.nl. Tour tickets 8.50€ adults, free for kids 10 and under. Online reservations required; times vary. Visitor Center open Tues–Sun 10am–5pm (mid-Nov to mid-Mar 11am–4pm). Closed Apr 27. Tram: 1 to Vredespaleis.*

The Peace Palace is a magnificent mock-Gothic home to the International Court of Justice.

The Hague Basics

The Hague is 50 minutes from Amsterdam's Centraal Station, and there are up to six trains an hour. A round-trip ticket is 22€. The Hague has two main rail stations, Den Haag Centraal Station and Den Haag HS; most sights are closer to Centraal Station, but some trains stop only at HS. Once you arrive at Den Haag Centraal Station, you'll find trams adjacent to the station. To get around, you can use an OV-chipkaart transit card or an HTM dagkaart (day ticket; 6.50€), which affords you unlimited use of public transportation in The Hague and Scheveningen.

Tourist information is at **VVV Den Haag,** Spui 68 (☎ **070/361-8860;** www.denhaag.nl), close to the Binnenhof (Parliament). It's open Monday from noon to 8pm, Tuesday to Friday from 10am to 8pm, Saturday from 10am to 5pm, and Sunday from noon to 5pm. Other tourist information points are at Lange Voorhout 58B (Tues–Sun 9am–5pm) and Wagenstraat 193 (Mon–Fri 9:30am–5pm; Sat 10am–5pm; and Sun 10am–2:30pm).

❹ ★★ **Scheveningen.** This relaxed beachside town is only a 15-minute tram ride from the center of The Hague. It has a wide, sandy beach and a charming pier affording great views of the North Sea. Seafood restaurants line the waterfront boardwalk, and on summer weekends, sun worshipers pack the beach. Towering over both the town and the beach is the majestic Steigenberger Kurhaus Hotel (see below), which is a good place for a drink or a snack with fine views of the sea. If you're in the mood for outdoor activity, take a long walk over the rolling sand dunes that dot the coast for miles. *Tram: 1, 9, or 11 to the beach; 10, 11, or 17 to the fishing harbor. The ride on trams 1 or 9 from Scheveningen back to Den Haag Centraal Station takes 20 min.*

Flying kites on the wide, sandy beach at Scheveningen.

Tourist Information in Scheveningen

Scheveningen has three tourist information points. The main office is at Boekhandel Scheveningen, Keizerstraat 50 (open Mon–Sat 9am–6pm). Another tourist bureau is in the NH Hotel Atlantic at Deltaplein 200 (daily 8am–11pm), and a third option is in Kantoor-boekhandel De Vulpen at Frederik Henderiklaan 179 (Mon, Wed, and Fri 9am–6pm, Tues 9am–7pm, Sat 9am–5pm, and Sun 1–5pm).

5 ★★★ **Steigenberger Kurhaus Hotel.** While in Scheveningen, stop for a drink and a mozzarella salad in the Conservatory and Terrace at the Steigenberger Kurhaus Hotel, which has views of the North Sea. If you're here on a cold afternoon, warm up with the traditional English-style high tea in the ultragracious Kurzaal restaurant. *Gevers Deynootplein 30.* ☎ *070/416-2636. www.kurhaus.nl. Conservatory and Terrace daily 10am–5pm; high tea daily 2:30–4:30pm. $$.*

6 ★ **kids Sea Life Scheveningen.** This large aquarium has a walk-through underwater tunnel that lets you observe the denizens of the deep, including sharks swimming above your head. ⏱ *1 hr. Strandweg 13.* ☎ *070/354-2100. www.visitsealife.com/scheveningen. Admission 16€ adults, 14€ people with disabilities, 11€ kids 3–11 (purchase online and save 2€ per ticket). Sept–June daily 10am–6pm; July–Aug daily 10am–8pm. Closed Dec 12 and 25. Tram: 1 or 9 to Kurhaus.*

7 ★★ **Museum Beelden aan Zee.** This quirky sculpture museum is built into the sand dunes, steps from Scheveningen's busy boardwalk. Take time to admire the construction and the use of natural light that spills into the main hall. Terraces overlooking the sea are strewn with sculptures, and indoor galleries look out over the sand dunes to the sea beyond. Most sculptures are of the human form and many are portraits, including an installation featuring the Dutch Royal Family. The collection numbers more than a thousand and is still growing. On the promenade outside the museum, Fairytale Sculptures by the Sea is a permanent installation that's free of charge; the cartoonlike figures are all by New Yorker Tom Otterness. ⏱ *90 min. Hartevelstraat 1 (off Gevers Deynootweg).* ☎ *070/358-5857. www.beeldenaanzee.nl. Admission 12€ adults, 6€ kids 13–18. Tues–Sun 10am–5pm. Closed Jan 1 and Dec 24, 25, and 31. Tram: 1 or 9 to Kurhaus.* ●

The outdoor sculpture garden at Beelden aan Zee.

The **Savvy Traveler**

Before You Go

Government Tourist Offices

For the U.S. & Canada: Netherlands Board of Tourism & Conventions (NBTC), 215 Park Avenue South, Suite 2005, New York, NY 10003 (☎ 212/370-7360; www.holland. com). **For the U.K. & Ireland:** No walk-in service. NBTC, Portland House, Bressenden Place, London SW1E 5RS (☎ 020/7539-7950; www.holland.com/uk). **In Holland:** Prinses Catharina-Amaliastraat 5, The Hague (Den Haag), (☎ 070/ 370-5705; www.nbtc.nl).

The Best Times to Go

"In season" in Amsterdam means from mid-April to mid-October. The peak of the tourist season is July and August, when the weather is at its finest. The climate in Amsterdam is never really extreme at any time of year, and if you're one of the growing numbers who favor shoulder- or off-season travel, you'll find the city every bit as attractive. Not only are airlines, hotels, and restaurants cheaper and less crowded during the off season (with more relaxed and personalized service), but there are also some very appealing events going on. You may want to go when the bulb fields west of Amsterdam are bursting with color from late March to mid-May, one of the best times to visit The Netherlands.

Festivals & Special Events

SPRING. Late March to mid-May, catch the **Opening of Keukenhof Gardens,** Lisse (see p 14). The greatest flower show on earth blooms with a spectacular display of tulips, narcissi, daffodils, hyacinths, bluebells, crocuses, lilies, amaryllis, and many other flowers at this 32-hectare (79-acre) garden in the heart of the bulb country.

There's said to be seven million bulbs planted, but who's counting? Contact **Keukenhof** (☎ 0252/465-555; www.keukenhof.nl).

During **Museum Weekend** in early April, most museums in Amsterdam and throughout The Netherlands offer free or reduced admission and have special exhibits. For more details, contact **Museumvereniging/Museumweekend** (☎ 020/512-8910; www.museumweekend.nl).

On April 27, Amsterdam celebrates **Koningsdag (King's Day),** a national holiday honoring King Willem-Alexander, with a gigantic dawn-to-dawn street party. The canals and central streets are jam-packed with celebrating hordes dressed up in orange clothes, daft hats, and bright orange wigs with Dutch flags waving everywhere. Street music and theater combine with lots of drinking during this good-natured if boisterous affair. *Tip:* Wear something orange, even if it's only an orange cap or an orange ribbon in your hair. Contact **Amsterdam Marketing** (☎ 020/ 706-6000; www.iamsterdam.com) for more information.

The second Saturday in May is **National Windmill Day** throughout The Netherlands. Around two-thirds of the country's almost 1,000 remaining working windmills open to the public; among them are Amsterdam's Molen van Sloten (☎ 020/669-0412; www.molenvansloten.nl) and the windmills at Zaanse Schans (☎ 075/681-0000; www.dezaanseschans.nl). Contact **De Hollandsche Molen** (☎ 020/ 623-8703; www.molens.nl).

SUMMER. From May through August, catch a performance at the

Previous page: Amsterdam's bustling Centraal Station.

Vondelpark Open-Air Theater (see p 117). Everything happens here: theater, all kinds of music (including full-scale classical concerts by the famed Royal Concertgebouw Orchestra), dance, and even operettas. Contact **Vondelpark Openluchttheater** (☎ 020/428-3360; www.openluchttheater.nl).

In the third week of June, **Open Garden Days** is your chance to find out what the fancy gardens behind the gables of some of the city's houses-turned-museums look like. A number of the best gardens are open to the public for 3 days. Contact **Grachten Musea** (☎ 020/320-3660; www.grachtenmusea.nl) for more information.

The **Amsterdam Roots Festival,** which runs for 5 days at the beginning of July at various venues around town, features world music and dance, along with workshops, films, and exhibits. The festival culminates in **Roots Open Air,** a multicultural feast of song and dance held at Oosterpark in Amsterdam-Oost (East). Contact **Amsterdam Roots Festival** (☎ 020/531-8181; amsterdamroots.nl).

One of the world's leading gatherings of top international jazz and blues musicians, the **North Sea Jazz Festival** unfolds over 3 concert-packed mid-July days at Rotterdam's giant Ahoy venue. Last-minute tickets are scarce, so book as far ahead as possible. Contact **North Sea Jazz Festival** (☎ 015/214-8393; www.northseajazz.com).

Europe's most gay-friendly city hosts the **Amsterdam Gay Pride** event over 3 days in early August. A crowd of 150,000 people turns out to watch the highlight Canal Parade, in which some 100 outrageously decorated boats cruise the canals. In addition, there are street discos, open-air theater performances, a sports program, and a film festival. Go to the website of

Amsterdam Gay Pride (www. amsterdamgaypride.nl) for more information.

The 10-day classical music **Grachtenfestival (Canals Festival)** plays in mid-August at various intimate and elegant venues along the canals and at the Muziekgebouw aan 't IJ. Closing out the festival is the exuberant Prinsengracht Concert, which is presented on a pontoon in front of the Hotel Pulitzer (see p 132). Contact **Stichting Grachtenfestival** (☎ 020/421-4542; www.grachtenfestival.nl) for more information.

Amsterdam previews its cultural season with the **Uitmarkt,** usually the last weekend in August. A 3-day "open information market" runs alongside free performances of music, opera, dance, theater, and cabaret at theaters, concert halls, and impromptu outdoor venues in the city. Go to the **Uitmarkt** website (www.uitmarkt.nl) for more information.

FALL. During **Open Monumentendag,** on the second Saturday in September, you have a chance to see historical buildings and monuments that are usually not open to the public—and to get in free as well. Contact **Stichting Open Monumentendag** (☎ 020/422-2118; www.openmonumentendag.nl) for more information.

On the third Sunday in September, starting at noon, participants in the popular **Dam tot Damloop (Dam to Dam Run),** start at the Dam in the center of Amsterdam, head out of town through the IJ Tunnel to the center of Zaandam, and return to the Dam, for a distance of 16km (10 miles). Contact **Dam tot Damloop** (☎ 072/533-8136; www.damloop.nl/en) for more information.

On the third Tuesday in September, King Willem-Alexander rides in a splendid gold coach to the Ridderzaal (Hall of the Knights)

in The Hague for the **State Opening of Parliament,** which opens the legislative session. Contact **VVV Den Haag** (☎ 070/361-8860; www.denhaag.nl) for more information.

WINTER. Sinterklaas, Holland's equivalent of Santa Claus (St. Nicholas), launches the Christmas season on the third Saturday of November, when he arrives in the city by boat at the Centraal Station pier. Accompanied by black-painted assistants called *Zwarte Piet* (Black Peter), who hand out candy to kids along the way, he goes in stately horseback procession through Amsterdam before being given the keys to the city by the mayor at the Dam. Contact the tourist office **Amsterdam Marketing** (☎ 020/702-6000; www.iamsterdam.com) for more information.

The city's **New Year's** celebrations take place throughout the city center on the night of December 31 to January 1, but mostly at the Dam and Nieuwmarkt. Things can get wild and not always so wonderful. Many of Amsterdam's youthful spirits celebrate the New Year with firecrackers, which they throw at the feet of passers-by. This keeps hospital emergency departments busy.

More than 300 indie films are screened at theaters around town during the **International Film Festival Rotterdam,** from late January to early February. Contact (☎ 010/890-9090; www.filmfestivalrotterdam.com) for more information.

The Weather

Summers are largely sunny, warm, and pleasant, with only a few oppressively hot days. Rain is common throughout the year, especially in winter.

Useful Websites

- **www.iamsterdam.com**, the city's excellent tourist office's website, is a virtually inexhaustible resource.
- **www.visitholland.com** offers comprehensive information,

covering hotels, sightseeing, and notices of special events.

- **www.amsterdamhotspots.nl** lists the latest places to see and be seen in the city.
- **www.dutchamsterdam.nl** is loaded with information about what's happening in the city.
- **www.amsterdam.info** has lots of practical information about the city.

Cellphones (Mobile Phones)

Most cellphones now have GSM (Global System for Mobiles) capability and you should be able to make and receive calls in The Netherlands. Mobile coverage is good all over the city. You can buy pre-paid SIM cards from several stores on Rokin. Alternatively, you can rent a phone through **Cellhire** (www.cellhire.com). After a simple online registration, they will ship a phone (usually with a U.K. number) to your home or office. Usage charges can be astronomical, so read the fine print. Cellphones can be hired from Telecom Rentcenter in Schiphol Plaza at the airport.

U.K. mobiles work in The Netherlands but roaming charges can be high. You are also charged for calls you *receive* on a U.K. mobile used abroad.

Car Rentals

There's no point in hiring a car in Amsterdam as the public transport system works efficiently and most attractions are within walking distance of each other. The roads are tiny, often one-way, some pedestrianized, and all are crowded with mad cyclists, but if you're traveling outside the city, it's usually cheapest to book a car online before you leave home. Try **Hertz** (www.hertz.com), **Avis** (www.avis.com), **Budget** (www.budget.com), or **Europcar** (www.europcar.com).

AMSTERDAM'S AVERAGE MONTHLY TEMPERATURES											
	JAN	FEB	MAR	APR	MAY	JUNE	JULY	AUG	SEPT	OCT	NOV	DEC
Temp. (°F)	38	39	43	47	54	59	63	62	58	52	44	40
Temp. (°C)	3	4	6	8	12	15	17	17	15	11	7	4

Getting **There**

By Plane
Arriving: Amsterdam Airport Schiphol (☎ 0900/0141 for general and flight information, 31-20/794-0800 from outside Holland; www.schiphol.nl; airport code AMS), 14km (9 miles) southwest of the city center, is the main airport in The Netherlands, handling the country's international arrivals and departures. Frequent travelers regularly vote Schiphol (pronounced *Skhip*-ol) one of the world's best airports for its ease of use; its massive, duty-free shopping center; and its branch of the Rijksmuseum.

After you deplane at one of the three terminals (all close together and numbered 1, 2, and 3), moving walkways take you to the Arrivals Hall, where you pass through Passport Control, Baggage Reclaim, and Customs. Conveniences such as free luggage carts (baggage trolleys), currency exchange, ATMs, restaurants, bars, shops, baby rooms, restrooms, and showers are available. Beyond these is Schiphol Plaza, which combines rail station access, the Yotel Schiphol Airport for transit passengers, a mall (sporting that most essential Dutch service—a flower store), bars and restaurants, restrooms, baggage lockers, airport and tourist information desks, car-rental and hotel-reservation desks, and more, all in a single location. Bus and shuttle stops and a taxi stand are just outside.

For tourist information and to make hotel reservations, go to the **Holland Tourist Information** desk in Schiphol Plaza (☎ 020/702-6000); it is open daily from 7am to 10pm.

Getting into town: Netherlands Railways (NS) **trains** (☎ 0900/9292; www.ns.nl) depart from Schiphol Station to Amsterdam Centraal Station downstairs from Schiphol Plaza; trains stop at De Lelylaan and De Vlugtlaan stations in west Amsterdam on the way. Frequency ranges from six trains an hour at peak times to one an hour at night. The fare is 4€ one-way; the ride takes 15 to 20 minutes.

An alternative rail route serves both Amsterdam Zuid station and Amsterdam RAI station (beside the RAI Convention Center). If you're staying at a hotel near Leidseplein, Rembrandtplein, in the Museum District, or in Amsterdam South, this route may be a better bet for you than Centraal Station. The fare is 2.50€ one-way; the ride takes around 15 minutes. From Zuid, take tram no. 5 for Leidseplein and the Museum District; from Amsterdam RAI, take tram no. 4 for Rembrandtplein.

The **Connexxion Schiphol Hotel Shuttle** (☎ +31 88/339-4741; www.schipholhotelshuttle.nl) runs between the airport and Amsterdam, serving around 100 hotels. The fare is 17€ one-way and 27€ round-trip; kids ages 4 to 14 pay 8€ and 13€. No reservations are needed and buses depart from in front of Schiphol Plaza every 10 to 30 minutes daily from 6am to 9pm. The bus ride takes anywhere from 40 to 90 minutes.

The **Connexxion bus no. 197** departs every 15 minutes or so from in front of Schiphol Plaza for Amsterdam's downtown Marnixstraat bus station (the line number is N97 at night, and the frequency is hourly), stopping in Museumplein and near Leidseplein on the way. The fare is 4€ and the trip takes about 40 minutes.

You'll find **taxis** waiting at the stand of **SchipholTaxi** (☎ 0900/900-6666; www.schipholtaxi.nl) in front of Schiphol Plaza. Taxis from the airport are metered. Expect to pay 45€ to 55€ to the center of Amsterdam; the ride takes 35 to 45 minutes. A service charge is already included in the fare.

By Boat from Britain

DFDS Seaways (☎ 0871/522-9955 in Britain, +44/330-333-0245 outside the U.K.; www.dfdsseaways.co.uk) has daily car-ferry service between Newcastle in northeast England and IJmuiden on the North Sea coast west of Amsterdam. The overnight travel time is 15½ hours. From IJmuiden, you can go by bus to Amsterdam Centraal Station.

P&O Ferries (☎ 08716/642121 in Britain, 020/200-8333 in Holland; www.poferries.com) has daily car-ferry service between Hull in northeast England and Rotterdam Europoort. The overnight travel time is 10 to 11 hours. Ferry-company buses shuttle passengers between the Europoort terminal and Rotterdam Centraal Station, from where there are frequent trains to Amsterdam.

Stena Line (☎ 08447/707070 in Britain; www.stenaline.co.uk) has a twice-daily car-ferry service between Harwich in southeast England and Hoek van Holland (Hook of Holland) near Rotterdam. The travel time is 6¾ hours for the daytime crossing, and 7½ hours for the overnight. Frequent trains depart from Hoek van Holland to Amsterdam.

By Cruise Ship

Cruise ship passengers arrive in Amsterdam at the **Passenger Terminal Amsterdam** (see p 40), Piet Heinkade 27 (☎ 020/509-1000; www.ptamsterdam.nl; tram 26), on the IJ waterway within easy walking distance of Centraal Station.

By Train

Rail services to Amsterdam from other cities in The Netherlands and elsewhere in Europe are frequent and fast. International trains arrive at Centraal Station from Brussels, Paris, Berlin, Cologne, and other German cities, and from more cities in Austria, Switzerland, Italy, and Eastern Europe. **Nederlandse Spoorwegen** (Netherlands Railways; www.ns.nl) trains arrive in Amsterdam from towns and cities all over The Netherlands. Service is frequent to many places around the country and trains are modern, clean, and punctual. Schedule and fare information on travel by train is available by calling ☎ 0900/9292 (0.70€ per minute) for national service and 0900/9296 for high-speed international services (0.35€ per minute), or by visiting www.ns.nl.

The burgundy-colored **Thalys** (www.thalys.com) high-speed train, with a top speed of 300kmph (186 mph), connects Paris, Brussels, Amsterdam, and (via Brussels) Cologne. Travel time from Paris to Amsterdam is 3 hours, 20 minutes, and from Brussels, 1 hour, 50 minutes. For Thalys information and reservations, call ☎ 3635 in France (0.35€ per minute); ☎ 070/797-979 in Belgium (0.30€ per minute); ☎ 8/9235-3536 in Germany; and ☎ 0900/9296 in The Netherlands. Tickets are also available from railway stations and travel agents.

On the **Eurostar** (www.eurostar.com) high-speed train (top speed 300kmph/186 mph), the travel time between London St. Pancras Station and Brussels's Bruxelles-Midi Station (the closest connecting point for Amsterdam) is around 2 hours. Departures from London to Brussels are approximately every 2 hours at peak times. For Eurostar reservations, call ☎ 08432/186186 in Britain or +44/1233-617-575 from outside the U.K.

Arriving at Centraal Station: Regardless of where they originate, most visitors traveling to Amsterdam by train find themselves deposited at Amsterdam's Centraal Station, built from 1884 to 1889 on an artificial island in the IJ channel. The building, an ornate architectural wonder on its own (see p 29), is the focus of much activity. It's at the hub of the city's concentric rings of canals and connecting main streets, and is the originating point for most of the city's trams, Metro trains, and buses.

You'll find an I amsterdam Visitor Information Centre right in front of the station at Stationsplein 10; the office has hotel-reservation desks. Other station facilities include a GWK Travelex Western Union currency-exchange office, ATMs, a service center for travel information and tickets, luggage lockers, restaurants and snack bars, newsstands, and specialty stores.

Warning: Centraal Station is home to a pickpocket convention that's in full swing at all times. Messages broadcast in multiple languages warn people to be on their guard, but the artful dodgers still seem to do good business. Avoid becoming one of their victims by keeping your money and other valuables under wraps, especially among crowds.

An array of tram stops are on either side of the main station exit—virtually all of Amsterdam's hotels are within a 15-minute tram ride from Centraal Station. The Metro station is downstairs, just outside the main exit. City bus stops are to the left of the main exit, and the taxi stands are to the right. At the public transportation GVB Tickets & Info office on Stationsplein, you can buy cards for trams, Metro trains, and buses (see "Getting Around," below, for more information). The station is also a departure point for passenger ferries across the IJ waterway, water taxis, canal-boat tours, the Museum Line boats, and the Canal Bus.

By Bus
International coaches—and in particular those of Eurolines—arrive at the bus terminal opposite the Amstel rail station (Metro: Amstel) in the south of the city. Eurolines operates coach service between London Victoria Bus Station and Amstel Station (via ferry), with up to five departures daily in the summer. Travel time is just over 12 hours. For reservations, contact **Eurolines** (☎ 08717/818178 in Britain or +31/88-076-1700 in Holland; www.eurolines.com). From here, you can go by train or Metro train to Centraal Station, or by tram no. 12 to the Museumplein area and to connecting points for trams to the city center. For the Leidseplein area, take the Metro toward Centraal Station, get out at Weesperplein, and go above ground to take tram 7 or 10.

By Car
A network of major international highways crisscrosses The Netherlands. European expressways E19, E35, and E231, converge on Amsterdam from France and Belgium to the south and from Germany to the north and east. These roads also have Dutch designations; as you approach the city they are, respectively, A4, A2, and A1. Amsterdam's ring road is A10. Distances between destinations are relatively short. Traffic is invariably heavy, but road conditions are otherwise excellent, service stations are plentiful, and highways are plainly signposted.

Getting **Around**

By Public Transportation

Most public transportation in The Netherlands uses an electronic stored-value card called the **OV-chipkaart.** There are four main types of OV-chipkaart: "personal" cards that can be used only by their pictured owner, "anonymous" cards that can be used by anyone, "disposable" cards, and "business" cards. The personal and anonymous cards, both valid for 5 years, cost 7.50€ and can be loaded and reloaded with up to 50€. Reduced-rate cards are available for seniors and children. Electronic readers on Metro and train station platforms and onboard trams and buses deduct the correct fare; just hold your card up against the reader at both the start and the end of the ride. *Remember:* These cards are valid not just in Amsterdam, but also everywhere in The Netherlands, no matter where you buy them or use them.

A better bet for short-term visitors who plan to use public transportation a lot is a 1-day or multiday card from GVB: 24 hours (7.50€), 48 hours (12€), 72 hours (17€), 96 hours (21€), 120 hours (26€), 144 hours (30€), and 168 hours (32€).

The central information and ticket sales point for GVB Amsterdam, the city's public transportation company, is **GVB Tickets & Info,** Stationsplein (☎ 0900/8011 for timetable and fare information and other customer services; www.gvb.nl), in front of Centraal Station, open Monday to Friday from 7am to 9pm, Saturday and Sunday from 8am to 9pm. In addition, cards are available from GVB and Netherlands Railways ticket booths in Metro and train stations, ticket machines (automats) at Metro and train stations, and ticket machines onboard some trams.

By Tram: Half the fun of Amsterdam is walking along the canals. The other half is riding the blue-and-gray trams that roll through most major streets. There are 15 tram routes, 10 of which (lines 1, 2, 4, 5, 9, 13, 16, 17, 24, and 26) begin and end at Centraal Station, so you know you can always get back to that central point if you get lost and have to start over. The city's other tram lines are 3, 7, 10, 12, and 14.

Most trams have just one available access door that opens automatically; you board toward the rear (in the case of the oldest trams, at the rear) following arrowed indicators that point the way to the door. To board a tram that has no such arrowed indicators, push the button on the outside of the car beside any door. To get off, you may need to push a button with an "open-door" graphic or the words DEUR OPEN. Tram doors close automatically, and they do it quite quickly, so don't hang around. Always remember to hold your card against the reader as you get on and off the tram.

By Bus: An extensive bus network complements the trams. Many bus routes begin and end at Centraal Station. It's generally faster to go by tram if you have the option, but some points in the city are served only by bus.

By Metro: The Metro can't compare to the labyrinthine systems of Paris, London, and New York, but Amsterdam does have its own Metro, with four lines—50, 51, 53, and 54—that run partly overground and bring people in from the suburbs and take them home again, running between 6am and midnight daily. You may want to take them simply as a sightseeing excursion, though to be frank, few of the sights on the lines are worth going out of your way for. From Centraal Station, you can use Metro trains to reach both Nieuwmarkt and Waterlooplein in the old city center.

The new Metro line 52, the Noord-Zuidlijn, is currently under construction to link Amsterdam-Noord (North), under the IJ waterway, with the city center and then Amsterdam Zuid station. It's due to be completed in 2017.

By Ferry: Free GVB ferries (gvb.nl) for passengers and two-wheel transportation connect the city center with Amsterdam-Noord (North), across the IJ waterway. The short crossings are free, which makes them ideal micro-cruises as they afford fine views of the harbor. Ferries depart from Waterplein West behind Centraal Station. One route goes to Buiksloterweg on the north shore, with ferries every 6 to 12 minutes round-the-clock. A second route goes to IJplein, a more easterly point on the north shore, with ferries every 8 to 15 minutes from 6:30am to around midnight. A third ferry goes west to NDSM-Werf, a 14-minute trip that affords a decent view of the harbor. A fourth ferry runs between the Azartplein on Java/KNSM Island to the east of Centraal Station and Zamenhofstraat on Noord.

By Water Bus: Two different companies operate water buses (rarely, if ever, used by locals) that ply the canals and waterways to the city's museums, attractions, and shopping and entertainment districts.

Canal Bus (☎ 020/217-0500; www.canal.nl) has three routes—Green, Red, and Orange—with stops that include Centraal Station, Westermarkt, Leidseplein, Rijksmuseum (with an extension to the RAI Convention Center when big shows are on there), and Waterlooplein. Hours of operation are daily from 9:25am to 7pm, with two buses an hour at peak times. A day pass that affords discounted admission to some museums and attractions is 20€ for adults, and 10€ for kids ages 4 to 12.

The **Museum Line** (☎ 020/530-1090; www.lovers.nl) boats transport weary visitors on their pilgrimages from museum to museum and have the added benefit of providing some of the features of a canal-boat cruise. Boats depart from the Rederij Lovers dock in front of Centraal Station daily from 10am to 6:45pm, every 30 minutes in summer and every 45 minutes in winter. They stop at key spots around town, providing access to museums and other sights. These include the Rijksmuseum, Van Gogh Museum, Stedelijk Museum, Anne Frank Huis, Museum Het Rembrandthuis, and Jewish Historical Museum. A ticket is 21€ for adults, and 11€ for kids ages 4 to 12. Tickets include discounted admission to some museums and attractions.

By Taxi

It used to be that you couldn't simply hail a cab from the street in Amsterdam, but nowadays they often stop if you do. Otherwise, find one of the taxi stands sprinkled around the city, generally near the luxury hotels; at major squares such as the Dam, Spui, Rembrandtplein, Westermarkt, and Leidseplein; and of course at Centraal Station. Taxis have rooftop signs and blue license plates, and are metered. Hotel reception staff can easily order a cab for you, too.

Fares are regulated citywide and all cabs are metered; the meter starts at 3€ and there is a charge of 2€ per kilometer. A generally reliable service is **Taxi Centrale Amsterdam (TCA;** ☎ 020/650-6506; www.tcataxi.nl). The fare includes a tip, but you may round up or give something for an extra service, like help with your luggage, or for a helpful chat.

By Water Taxi

Since you're in the city of canals, you might like to splurge on a water taxi. These launches do more or less the same thing as landlubber taxis, except that they do it on the canals and the Amstel River and in the harbor. You can move faster than on land and you get your very own canal cruise. To order one, call **VIP Watertaxi** (☎ 020/535-6369; www.water-taxi.nl), or pick up from the dock outside Centraal Station, close to the VVV office. For up to eight people, the fare is 10€ for 30 minutes in the city center, and 50€ for 30 minutes outside the city center.

By Bike

Instead of renting a car, follow the Dutch example and ride a bicycle. Sunday, when the city is quiet, is a particularly good day to pedal through Vondelpark and along off-the-beaten-path canals, or to practice riding on cobblestones and in bike lanes, crossing bridges, and dodging trams before venturing forth into the fray of an Amsterdam rush hour. There are more than 600,000 bikes in the city, so you'll have plenty of company.

Navigating the city on two wheels is mostly safe—or at any rate not as suicidal as it looks—thanks to a vast network of dedicated bike lanes. Bikes even have

their own traffic lights. Amsterdam's battle-scarred bike-borne veterans make it almost a point of principle to ignore every safety rule ever written. Although they mostly live to tell the tale, don't think the same will necessarily apply to you.

Bike rental rates start at 13€ a day at **MacBike** (☎ 020/428-1400; www.macbike.nl), which rents a range of bikes, including tandems and six-speed touring bikes, and has rental outlets at Stationsplein 5 outside Centraal Station, Oosterdokskade 149, Weteringschans 2 at Leidseplein, Marnixstraat 220, and Waterlooplein 199. Open Monday through Saturday 9am to 5:45pm and Sunday noon to 6pm.

Warning: Always lock both your bike frame and one of the wheels to something solid and fixed, because theft is common.

By Car

Driving in Amsterdam is not recommended. Parking is difficult, traffic is dense, and networks of one-way streets make navigation, even with the best of maps, a problem. You would be much better advised to make use of the city's extensive public transportation or to take cabs.

By Foot

The best way to take in the city is to walk, and the city center is pedestrian-friendly. Carry a good map with you, and watch out for those ubiquitous speeding bikes and speeding trams.

Fast **Facts**

ATMS The easiest and best way to get cash abroad is through an ATM; the **Cirrus** and **Plus** networks span the globe. Most banks charge a fee for international withdrawals—check with your bank before

you leave home and find out your daily limit. There are many ATMs in Amsterdam, and in the center of town you'll be virtually tripping over the things. Many of them are open 24/7, although you'll want to be a bit cautious about withdrawing cash in quiet areas after dark.

BABYSITTERS Many mid- and upper-range Amsterdam hotels can arrange babysitting services. A reliable local organization is **Oppascentrale Kriterion** (☎ 020/624-5848; www.oppascentralekriterion.nl), which has vetted babysitters over 18. Its rates are 7€ an hour for a minimum of 3 hours, plus a 5€ administration charge per booking, and a minimum charge of 21€; a possible deal-breaker is the 25€ registration fee.

BANKS Among the leading Dutch banks, ABN AMRO (www.abnamro.nl), ING (www.ing.com), Rabobank (www.rabobank.nl), and SNS (www.snsbank.nl) all have multiple branches around Amsterdam. Most banks are open Monday to Friday from 9am to 5:30pm (some stay open Thurs until 7pm). A few are open on Saturday morning.

BIKE RENTALS See "By Bike," under "Getting Around," earlier in this chapter.

BUSINESS HOURS Shops tend to be open from 9:30am to 6pm Tuesday, Wednesday, Friday, and Saturday. Some stay open until 8 or 9pm on Thursday. Many close on Monday morning, opening at 1pm, and most stores outside the center will close all day Sunday. Most museums close 1 day a week (often Monday), but may be open some holidays, except Koningsdag (King's Day on April 27), Christmas, and New Year's Day.

CONSULATES & EMBASSIES U.K. Consulate: Koningslaan 44 (☎ 020/676-4343; www.britain.nl; tram 2). **U.S. Consulate:** Museumplein 19 (☎ 020/575-5330; amsterdam.usconsulate.gov; tram 3, 5, 12, 16, or 24).

Embassies are in The Hague (Den Haag): **Australian Embassy,** Carnegielaan 4 (☎ 070/310-8200; www.netherlands.embassy.gov.au); **Canadian Embassy,** Sophialaan 7

(☎ 070/311-1600; netherlands.gc.ca); **Irish Embassy,** Scheveningseweg 112 (☎ 070/363-0993; www.irishembassy.nl); **New Zealand Embassy,** Eisenhowerlaan 77N (☎ 070/346-9324; www.nzembassy.com/netherlands); **U.K. Embassy,** Lange Voorhout 10 (☎ 070/427-0427; www.britain.nl); **U.S. Embassy,** Lange Voorhout 102 (☎ 070/310-2209; thehague.usembassy.gov).

CREDIT CARDS In The Netherlands, you'll rarely come across a business that uses the old swipe system for authorizing credit card payments. Instead, payments will either be authorized by a chip system in the card and the cardholder's signature, or by chip-and-PIN, with a four-digit personal identification number replacing the signature. You can withdraw cash advances from your credit cards at banks or ATMs provided you know your PIN. Keep in mind that when you use your credit card abroad, most banks assess a 2% fee above the 1% fee charged by Visa, Master-Card, and American Express. You also pay interest from the day of your withdrawal, even if you pay your monthly bill on time.

CURRENCY EXCHANGE Few people now carry travelers' checks, but they can be cashed at foreign-exchange offices, not at banks, shops, or hotels. Currency exchanges are found at Amsterdam's Schiphol Airport and Centraal Station.

CUSTOMS Travelers arriving from a **non–European Union country** can bring in, duty-free, 200 cigarettes (or 250g of tobacco), or 100 cigarillos (or 50 cigars); 1 liter of alcohol over 22 proof, or 2 liters under 22 proof, 4 liters of wine, and 16 liters of beer; and 50ml of perfume or 0.25 liters of eau de toilette. Travelers arriving from an **E.U. country** can bring any amount of goods into The Netherlands, so long as they are intended for personal use and not for resale;

there are generous guideline limits, beyond which the goods may be deemed to be for resale.

DENTISTS See "Emergencies," below.

DOCTORS See "Emergencies," below.

DRUGSTORES In The Netherlands, a pharmacy is called an *apotheek* and sells both prescription and nonprescription medicines. Regular hours are Monday to Saturday from around 9am to 6pm. A centrally located pharmacy is **Dam Apotheek,** Damstraat 2 (☎ 020/624-4331; www.dam-apotheek.nl; tram 4, 9, 14, 16, or 24), close to the Nationaal Monument on the Dam. Pharmacies post details of nearby all-night and Sunday pharmacies on their doors.

EMERGENCIES For any emergency (fire, police, ambulance), the number is ☎ 112 from any land line or cellphone. For 24-hour urgent but nonemergency medical or dental services, call ☎ 088/0030-600; the operator will connect you to an appropriate doctor or dentist. To report a theft, call ☎ 0900/8844. **Residents of an E.U. country** must have a European Health Insurance Card (EHIC) to receive full reciprocal health-care benefits in The Netherlands.

EVENT LISTINGS A-mag is Amsterdam's cool new listings magazine, published bi-monthly in English. It lists all the happenings around town and is available at newsstands for 3€. It may be picked up for free in some hotels, too. The website www.iamsterdam.com is also an excellent source of what's on where.

FAMILY TRAVEL The I amsterdam website has a family travel section that's very helpful: www.iamsterdam.com/en-GB/experience/for-you/families-and-children.

GAY & LESBIAN TRAVEL COC Amsterdam, Rozenstraat 14 (☎ 020/626-3087; www.cocamsterdam.nl), is the local branch of the Dutch LGBT organization. It can answer any questions about anything gay in The Netherlands. The city's largest gay and lesbian bookstore is **Boekhandel Vrolijk,** Paleisstraat 135 (☎ 020/623-5142; www.vrolijk.nu).

HOLIDAYS National holidays include New Year's Day (Jan 1), Good Friday, Easter Sunday, and Easter Monday (Mar or Apr), King's Day (Apr 27), Liberation Day (May 5), Ascension Day (40 days after Easter), Pentecost Sunday (seventh Sun after Easter) and Pentecost Monday, Christmas Day (Dec 25), and Dec 26.

INSURANCE North Americans with homeowner's or renter's insurance are probably covered for lost luggage. If not, inquire with **Travel Assistance International** (☎ 800/643-5525; www.travelassistance.com) or **Travelex** (☎ 800/228-9792; www.travelexinsurance.com), insurers that can also provide trip-cancellation, medical, and emergency evacuation coverage abroad. **For U.K. and Irish citizens,** insurance is always advisable, even if you have a European Health Insurance Card (EHIC, see "Emergencies," above). The website www.moneysupermarket.com compares prices across a wide range of providers for single- and multitrip policies.

INTERNET ACCESS Most hotels in Amsterdam offer WiFi access. KPN hotspots are scattered throughout the city; cost is from 1.50€ for 15 minutes (portal.hotspotsvankpn.com).

LIQUOR LAWS Supermarkets, grocery stores, and cafes sell alcoholic beverages. The legal drinking age is 18, or 16 if the alcohol is under 15% proof.

LOST PROPERTY If your luggage is lost, immediately file a lost-luggage claim at the airport, detailing the luggage contents; and call lost and found (☎ 020/794-0800), open daily 7am to 6pm. For most airlines, you must report delayed, damaged, or lost baggage within 4 hours of arrival.

MAIL & POST OFFICES Amsterdam no longer has post offices as such; instead, various branches of newsagents, supermarkets, and grocery stores have postal points run by **PostNL** (www.post.nl). The stationers Gebroeders Winter (Rozengracht 62), the branch of Albert Heijn supermarket at Jodenbreestraat 21, and the Ako newsstand (Reguliersbreestraat 19) all have postal points where you can mail a parcel or postcards home. Stamps can also be purchased from your hotel reception and any newsstands that sell postcards.

MONEY The currency of The Netherlands is the euro, which can also be used in most other E.U. countries. The exchange rate varies, but at press time, 1 euro was equal to around US$1.38 and 0.82£. The best way to get cash in Amsterdam is at ATMs (see above). Credit cards are accepted at almost all hotels and many shops and restaurants, but you should always have some cash on hand for incidentals.

NEWSPAPERS & MAGAZINES Most kiosks sell English-language newspapers, including the *International Herald Tribune, USA Today*, and British papers such as *The Times* and *The Guardian*.

PASSPORTS If your passport is lost or stolen, contact your country's embassy or consulate immediately (see "Consulates & Embassies," above). Before you travel, you should copy the critical pages and keep them separately from your passport.

POLICE Call ☎ 112 for emergencies or ☎ 0900/8844 to report a theft. The most central police station is at Lijnbaansgracht 219 (☎ 0900/8844; tram 1, 2, 5, 7, or 10), just off Leidseplein.

SAFETY Be especially aware of child pickpockets. Their method is to get very close to a target, ask for a handout, and deftly help themselves to your money or passport. Robbery at gun- or knifepoint is very rare but not unknown. For more information, consult the U.S. State Department's website at www.travel.state.gov; in the U.K., consult the Foreign Office's website, www.fco.gov.uk; and in Australia, consult the government travel advisory service at www.smar traveller.gov.au.

SENIOR TRAVELERS Mention that you're a senior when you make your travel reservations. As in most cities, people 60 and older (in some places it may be 65 and older), qualify for reduced admission to Amsterdam theaters, museums, and other attractions, as well as discounted fares on public transportation.

SMOKING Smoking is banned in all public places and on all public transportation. In some places, it is also banned in the streets. Ironically, it's also banned in coffee shops, although you can still smoke a joint.

TAXES Value-added tax, or VAT (BTW in The Netherlands), is standard at 21%, with a lower rate of 6% on some items. Non-E.U. visitors can get a refund if they spend 50€ or more in any store that participates in the VAT refund program. The shops will give you a form, which you must get stamped at Customs (allow extra time). Customs may ask to see your purchase, so don't pack it in your checked luggage. Mark the paperwork to request a credit card refund;

otherwise, you'll be stuck with a check in euros.

TELEPHONES Public phones are run by KPN Telecom and all take their own brand of prepaid chip cards or personal credit cards; there are virtually no coin-operated public phones left in Amsterdam. Look out for the bright green phone booths around main squares and the station. Prepaid KPN cards cost 5€, 10€, or 20€. For operator assistance, call ☎ 0800/0410. The country code for The Netherlands is +31; for Amsterdam, the city code is either 020 for landlines or 06 for mobiles. To make a **direct international call,** dial 00, then dial the country code, the area code, and the local number. The country code for the **U.S. and Canada** is 1; **Great Britain,** 44; **Ireland,** 353; **Australia,** 61; and **New Zealand,** 64. Beware of making international calls on your hotel phone as rates will be astronomical.

TICKETS The best outlet is the centrally located **Last Minute Ticket Shop** (see p 120) at the Stadsschouwburg, Leidseplein 26 (no phone; www.lastminuteticket shop.nl). You can buy tickets on this website prior to your arrival. Hotel concierges will normally book tickets for you, too.

TIPPING In cafes and restaurants, waiter service is usually included, though you can round the bill up or leave some small change if you like. A service charge is included in taxi fares, but a small tip (1€–2€) is always appreciated. If you make the driver wait or are going on a long, expensive trip, tip 5%. Tip hotel porters 1€ to 2€ for each piece of luggage.

TOILETS If you use a toilet at a brown cafe or restaurant, it's customary to make some small purchase, or leave .50€.

TOURIST OFFICES The main outlet is the tourist office of I amsterdam at Stationsplein 10, right outside Centraal Station (☎ 020/702-6000; www.iamsterdam.com). There's also a branch in Schiphol Plaza at the airport, with the same phone number.

TOURS Viator (☎ 702/648-5873; www.viator.com) offers a great selection of Amsterdam-based tours, from pub crawls to skip-the-line visits to the Rijksmuseum and day trips to see the tulips at Keukenhof.

TRAVELERS WITH DISABILITIES Nearly all modern hotels in Amsterdam now have rooms designed for people with disabilities, but many older, townhouse hotels do not even have elevators. Not all trams in Amsterdam are fully accessible for wheelchairs, but new trams have low central doors that are accessible. Amsterdam's Metro system is fully accessible.

Amsterdam: **A Brief History**

1200 Fishermen establish a settlement at the mouth of the Amstel River, which is subsequently dammed to control flooding; the settlement takes the name "Aemstelledamme."

1300 The bishop of Utrecht grants Amsterdam its first town charter.

1323 Amsterdam's economy receives a boost when it is declared a toll center for beer.

1350 The city becomes a transit point for imported grain, growing in importance as a trade center.

1602 The United East India Company (V.O.C.), destined to become a powerful force in Holland's Golden Age of discovery, exploration, and trade, is founded.

1611 First Amsterdam Stock Exchange opens.

1613 Construction begins on the Grachtengordel (Canal Ring), comprising the Herengracht, Keizersgracht, and Prinsengracht canals.

1631 Rembrandt, at age 25, moves to Amsterdam from his native Leiden.

1795 French troops occupy Holland with the aid of Dutch revolutionaries and establish the Batavian Republic; William V flees to England.

1806–10 Louis Bonaparte, Napoleon's brother, reigns as king of Holland.

1813 The Netherlands regains independence from the French.

1839 Holland's first rail line, connecting Amsterdam and Haarlem, opens.

1910 A flushable water system for the city's canals is introduced.

1920 Dutch airline KLM launches the world's first scheduled air service, between Amsterdam and London.

1928 The Olympics are held in Amsterdam.

1932 Afsluitdijk (Enclosure Dike) at the head of the Zuiderzee is completed, transforming the sea on which Amsterdam stands into the freshwater IJsselmeer lake.

1940 On May 10, Nazi Germany invades The Netherlands, which surrenders 4 days later.

1944–45 Thousands die during the Hunger Winter, when Nazi occupation forces blockade western Holland.

1945 On May 5, German forces in The Netherlands surrender.

1960s Amsterdam takes on the mantle of Europe's hippie capital.

1973 The Van Gogh Museum opens.

1975 Amsterdam's 700th anniversary. Cannabis use is decriminalized.

1987 The *Homomonument,* the world's first public memorial to persecuted gays and lesbians, is unveiled.

2001 The world's first same-sex marriage with a legal status identical to heterosexual matrimony takes place in Amsterdam.

2002 Euro bank notes and coins replace the guilder.

2004 Controversial film director Theo van Gogh is murdered by an Islamist extremist on the streets of Amsterdam.

2005 Homophobic assailants in Amsterdam beat up the editor of the *Washington Blade* LGBT newspaper.

2008 Smoking in restaurants, cafes, bars, and nightclubs is banned.

2010 The new Dutch coalition government announces plans to prevent foreign visitors from frequenting cannabis-selling coffee shops. This comes to nothing.

2013 Queen Beatrix abdicates and her son Willem-Alexander is inaugurated as king on April 30.

Golden Age Art

Although there were earlier prominent Dutch artists, Dutch art really came into its own during the 17th-century Golden Age. Artists were blessed with wealthy patrons whose support allowed them to give free rein to their talents. The primary art patrons were Protestant merchants who commissioned portraits, genre scenes, and still lifes, not the kind of religious works commissioned by the church in Catholic countries. The Dutch were particularly fond of pictures that depicted their world: landscapes, seascapes, domestic scenes, and portraits.

Gerrit van Honthorst (1590–1656)

A Utrecht artist who had studied in Rome with Caravaggio, Van Honthorst brought the new "realism of light and dark," or *chiaroscuro* technique, to Holland, where he influenced Dutch artists such as the young Rembrandt. Van Honthorst is best known for lively company scenes such as *The Supper Party* (ca. 1620; Uffizi, Florence), which depicted ordinary people against a plain background and set a style that continued in Dutch art for many years. He often used multiple hidden light sources to heighten the dramatic contrast of lights and darks.

Jacob van Ruisdael (1628–82)

Among the great landscape artists of this period, Van Ruisdael stands out. In his paintings, human figures either do not appear at all or are shown almost insignificantly small; vast skies filled with moody clouds often cover two-thirds of the canvas. His *Windmill at Wijk bij Duurstede* (ca. 1665; Rijksmuseum, Amsterdam) combines many characteristic elements of his style. The windmill stands in a somber landscape, containing a few small human figures, with a cloud-laden sky and a foreground of agitated water and reeds.

Frans Hals (ca. 1580–1666)

Antwerp-born Hals, the undisputed leader of the Haarlem school (schools differed from city to city), was a great portrait painter whose relaxed, informal, and naturalistic portraits contrast strikingly with the traditional formal masks of Renaissance portraits. His light brushstrokes help convey immediacy and intimacy, making his works perceptive psychological portraits. He had a genius for comic characters, showing men and women as they are and a little less than they are, as in *Malle Babbe* (ca. 1635; Gemäldegalerie, Berlin). As a stage designer of group portraits, Hals's skill is almost unmatched—only Rembrandt is superior. Although he carefully arranged and posed each group, balancing the directions of gesture and glance, his *alla prima* brushwork (direct laying down of pigment) makes these public images seem spontaneous. It's worth taking a day trip to Haarlem just to visit the Frans Hals Museum (see p 139) and view such works as his *A Banquet of the Officers of the St George Civic Guard* (ca. 1627) and *Officers and Sergeants of the St Hadrian Civic Guard* (ca. 1633).

Rembrandt (1606–69)

The great genius of the period was Rembrandt Harmenszoon van Rijn, one of few artists of any period to be known simply by his first name. This painter, whose works hang in places of honor in the world's great galleries, may be *the* most famous

Amsterdammer, both to outsiders and to today's city residents.

Rembrandt pushed the art of *chiaroscuro* to unprecedented heights. In his paintings, the values of light and dark gradually and softly blend together; this may have diffused some of the drama of *chiaroscuro*, but it achieved a more truthful appearance. His art seems capable of revealing the soul and inner life of his subjects, and to view his series of 60 self-portraits is to see a remarkable documentation of his own psychological and physical evolution. The etching *Self-Portrait with Saskia* (1636; Rijksmuseum, Amsterdam) shows him with his wife at a prosperous time when he was being commissioned to paint portraits of wealthy merchants. Later self-portraits are psychologically complex, often depicting a careworn old man whose gaze is nonetheless sharp, compassionate, and wise.

In group portraits like *The Night Watch* (1642) and *The Syndics of the Cloth Guild* (1662), both in the Rijksmuseum, each individual portrait is done with care. The unrivaled harmony of light, color, and movement of these works is a marvel to be appreciated. Compare, too, these robust, masculine works with the tender *The Jewish Bride* (ca. 1665), also in the Rijksmuseum.

In later years, Rembrandt was at the height of his artistic powers, but his contemporaries judged his work to be too personal and eccentric. Some considered him a tasteless painter who was obsessed with the ugly and ignorant of color; this opinion prevailed until the 19th century, when Rembrandt's genius was reevaluated.

Jan Vermeer (1632–75)

Perhaps the best known of the "little Dutch masters" who specialized in one genre of painting, such as portraiture, is Jan Vermeer of Delft. Although they confined their artistry within a narrow scope, these painters rendered their subjects with an exquisite care and faithfulness to their actual appearances.

Vermeer's work centers on the simple pleasures and activities of domestic life—a woman pouring milk or reading a letter, for example—and all of his simple figures positively glow with color and light. Vermeer placed the figure (usually just one, but sometimes two or more) at the center of his paintings against a background in which furnishings often provided the horizontal and vertical balance, giving the composition a feeling of stability and serenity. Art historians have determined that Vermeer used mirrors and the camera obscura, an optical projection device, as compositional aids. A master at lighting interior scenes and rendering true colors, Vermeer was able to create an illusion of three-dimensionality in works such as *The Love Letter* (ca. 1670; Rijksmuseum, Amsterdam). As light—usually afternoon sunshine pouring in from an open window—moves across the picture plane, it caresses and modifies all the colors.

Jan Steen (ca. 1626–79)

Born in Leiden, Steen painted marvelous interior scenes, often satirical and didactic in their intent. The allusions on which much of the satire depends may escape most of us today, but any viewer can appreciate the fine drawing, subtle color shading, and warm light that pervades such paintings as *Woman at Her Toilet* (1663) and *The Feast of St. Nicholas* (ca. 1665), both in the Rijksmuseum, Amsterdam. Many of his pictures revel in bawdy tavern scenes fueled by overindulgence in beer and gin.

Useful Phrases & Menu Terms

Useful Words & Phrases

ENGLISH	DUTCH	PRONUNCIATION
Hello	Dag/Hallo	*dakh*/ha-*loh*
Good morning	Goedenmorgen	khoo-*yuh*-mor-*khun*
Good afternoon/ evening	Goedenavond	khoo-*yuhn*-af-*ond*
How are you?	Hoe gaat het met u?	*hoo* khaht *et* met *oo*?
Very well	Uitstekend	*out*-stayk-*end*
Thank you	Dank u wel	*dahnk* oo wel
Goodbye	Dag/Tot ziens	*dakh*/tot *zeenss*
Good night	Goedenacht	khoo-*duh*-nakht
See you later	Tot straks	*Tot* strahkss
Please	Alstublieft	ahl-*stoo-bleeft*
Yes	Ja	*yah*
No	Neen/nee	*nay*
Excuse me	Pardon	*par*-dawn
Sorry	Sorry	so-*ree*
Do you speak English?	Spreekt u Engels?	*spraykt* oo eng-*els*
Can you help me?	Kunt u mij helpen?	*koont* oo may-ee hel-*pen*?
Give me . . .	Geeft u mij . . .	*khayft* oo may . . .
Where is . . . ?	Waar is . . . ?	*vahr iz* . . . ?
a bank	een bank	*ayn bank*
a hotel	een hotel	ayn ho-*tel*
a restaurant	een restaurant	ayn res-to-*rahng*
a pharmacy/chemist	een apotheek	ayn a-po-*tayk*
the post office	het postkantoor	het post-*kan-tohr*
the station	het station	het stah-*ssyonh*
the toilet	het toilet	het twah-*let*
To the right	Rechts	*rekhts*
To the left	Links	*links*
Straight ahead	Rechtdoor	*rekht*-doar
I would like . . .	Ik zou graag . . .	*ik zow khrakh* . . .
to eat	eten	ay-*ten*
a room for one night	een kamer voor een nacht willen	ayn *kah-mer voor* ayn *nakht* wi-*llen*
How much is it?	Hoe veel kost het?	*hoo fayl kawst het*
the check	de rekening	*duh* ray-ken-*ing*
When?	Wanneer?	*vah*-neer
yesterday	gisteren	*khis*-ter-*en*
today	vandaag	van-*dahkh*
tomorrow	morgen	*mor*-khen
breakfast	ontbijt	ohnt-*bayt*
lunch	lunch	*lunch*
dinner	diner	dee-*nay*

Numbers

ENGLISH	DUTCH	PRONUNCIATION
one	een	*ayn*
two	twee	*tway*
three	drie	*dree*
four	vier	*veer*
five	vijf	*vayf*
six	zes	*zes*
seven	zeven	*zay-vun*
eight	acht	*akht*
nine	negen	*nay-khen*
ten	tien	*teen*
eleven	elf	*elf*
twelve	twaalf	*tvahlf*
thirteen	dertien	*dayr-teen*
fourteen	veertien	*vayr-teen*
fifteen	vijftien	*vayf-teen*
sixteen	zestien	*zes-teen*
seventeen	zeventien	*zay-vun-teen*
eighteen	achttien	*akh-teen*
nineteen	negentien	*nay-khun-teen*
twenty	twintig	*twin-tikh*

Days of the Week

ENGLISH	DUTCH	PRONUNCIATION
Monday	Maandag	*mahn-dakh*
Tuesday	Dinsdag	*deens-dakh*
Wednesday	Woensdag	*voohns-dakh*
Thursday	Donderdag	*donder-dakh*
Friday	Vrijdag	*vray-dakh*
Saturday	Zaterdag	*zahter-dakh*
Sunday	Zondag	*zohn-dakh*

Months

ENGLISH	DUTCH	PRONUNCIATION
January	Januari	*yahn-oo-aree*
February	Februari	*fayhb-roo-aree*
March	Maart	*mahrt*
April	April	*ah-pril*
May	Mei	*meh-eey*
June	Juni	*yoo-nee*
July	Juli	*yoo-lee*
August	Augustus	*awh-khoost-oos*
September	September	*sep-tem-buhr*
October	Oktober	*oct-oah-buhr*
November	November	*noa-vem-buhr*
December	December	*day-sem-buhr*

Dutch Menu Savvy

BASICS

DUTCH	ENGLISH
ontbijt	breakfast
lunch	lunch
diner	dinner
voorgerechten	starters
hoofdgerechten	main courses
nagerechten	desserts
boter	butter
boterham	sandwich
brood	bread
stokbrood	French bread
honing	honey
hutspot	mashed potatoes and carrots, with onions
jam	jam
kaas	cheese
mosterd	mustard
pannenkoeken	pancakes
peper	pepper
zout	salt
suiker	sugar
saus	sauce

SOUPS (SOEPEN)

DUTCH	ENGLISH
soep	soup
aardappelsoep	potato soup
bonensoep	bean soup
erwtensoep	pea soup (usually includes bacon or sausage)
groentesoep	vegetable soup
kippensoep	chicken soup
uiensoep	onion soup
tomatensoep	tomato soup

EGGS (EIEREN)

DUTCH	ENGLISH
eier	egg
hardgekookte eieren	hard-boiled eggs
zachtgekookte eieren	soft-boiled eggs
omelette	omelet
roereieren	scrambled eggs
spiegeleieren	fried eggs
uitsmijter	fried eggs and ham on bread

FISH (VIS)

DUTCH	ENGLISH
forel	trout
garnalen	prawns
gerookte zalm	smoked salmon
haring	herring

DUTCH	ENGLISH
kabeljauw	cod
kreeft	lobster
makreel	mackerel
mosselen	mussels
oesters	oysters
paling	eel
sardientjes	sardines
schelvis	haddock
schol	plaice
tong	sole
zalm	salmon

MEATS (VLEES)

DUTCH	ENGLISH
rundvlees	beef
biefstuk	steak
eend	duck
fricandeau	roast pork
gans	goose
gehakt	minced meat
haasbiefstuk	filet steak
ham	ham
kalfsvlees	veal
kalkoen	turkey
kip	chicken
konijn	rabbit
lamsvlees	lamb
lamskotelet	lamb chops
ragout	beef stew
rookvlees	smoked meat
lever	liver
spek	bacon
vleeswaren	cold cuts
worst	sausage

VEGETABLES & SALADS (GROENTEN/SLA)

DUTCH	ENGLISH
groenten	vegetables
asperges	asparagus
augurken	pickles
bieten	beets
bloemkool	cauliflower
bonen	beans
champignons	mushrooms
erwten	peas
aardappelen	potatoes
knoflook	garlic
komkommer	cucumber
komkommersla	cucumber salad

DUTCH	ENGLISH
kool	cabbage
patates frites	french fries
prei	leek
prinsesseboonen	green beans
purée	mashed potatoes
radijsjes	radishes
rapen	turnips
rijst	rice
sla	lettuce, salad
spinazie	spinach
tomaten	tomatoes
uien	onions
wortelen	carrots
zuurkool	sauerkraut

DESSERTS (NAGERECHTEN)

DUTCH	ENGLISH
appelgebak	apple pie
appelmoes	applesauce
cake	cake
compote	stewed fruits
gebak	pastry/cake
ijs	ice cream
oliebollen	doughnuts
koekjes	cookies
jonge kaas	young cheese (mild)
oude kaas	mature cheese (strong)
room	cream
slagroom	whipped cream
smeerkaas	cheese spread
speculaas	spiced cookies

FRUITS (VRUCHTEN)

DUTCH	ENGLISH
aardbei	strawberry
ananas	pineapple
appel	apple
citroen	lemon
druiven	grapes
framboos	raspberry
kersen	cherries
peer	pear
perzik	peach
pruimen	plums

BEVERAGES (DRANKEN)

DUTCH	ENGLISH
bier (or pils)	beer
cognac	brandy
fles	bottle
glas	glass
jenever	gin
koffie	coffee
melk	milk
rode wijn	red wine
thee	tea
water	water
mineraal water	sparkling water
witte wijn	white wine

COOKING TERMS

DUTCH	ENGLISH
gebakken	baked/fried
gebraden	roast
gegrild	grilled
gekookt	boiled/cooked
gerookt	smoked
geroosterd	roasted/toasted
gestoofd	stewed/braised
goed doorbakken	well done
half doorbakken	medium
koud	cold
niet doorbakken	rare
warm	hot

Index

See also Accommodations and Restaurants & Cafes indexes, below.

Index

Photo **Credits**

Notes